Russian Military Wartime Personnel Recruiting and Retention 2022-2023

DARA MASSICOT

Prepared for the United States European Command
Approved for public release; distribution is unlimited

NATIONAL DEFENSE RESEARCH INSTITUTE

For more information on this publication, visit **www.rand.org/t/RRA2061-4**.

About RAND

The RAND Corporation is a research organization that develops solutions to public policy challenges to help make communities throughout the world safer and more secure, healthier and more prosperous. RAND is nonprofit, nonpartisan, and committed to the public interest. To learn more about RAND, visit www.rand.org.

Research Integrity

Our mission to help improve policy and decisionmaking through research and analysis is enabled through our core values of quality and objectivity and our unwavering commitment to the highest level of integrity and ethical behavior. To help ensure our research and analysis are rigorous, objective, and nonpartisan, we subject our research publications to a robust and exacting quality-assurance process; avoid both the appearance and reality of financial and other conflicts of interest through staff training, project screening, and a policy of mandatory disclosure; and pursue transparency in our research engagements through our commitment to the open publication of our research findings and recommendations, disclosure of the source of funding of published research, and policies to ensure intellectual independence. For more information, visit www.rand.org/about/principles.

RAND's publications do not necessarily reflect the opinions of its research clients and sponsors.

Published by the RAND Corporation, Santa Monica, Calif.
© 2024 RAND Corporation
RAND® is a registered trademark.

Library of Congress Cataloging-in-Publication Data is available for this publication.

ISBN: 978-1-9774-1327-7

Cover image by Nikolay Vinokurov/Alamy Stock Photo.

About This Report

This report presents an evaluation of the current and potential effects of Russia's full-scale 2022 invasion of Ukraine on Russian military manpower, recruiting, and retention. It builds on previously published RAND analysis of Russian military personnel policies for recruiting, retention, and proficiency from 1991 to 2021. This report presents a survey of the severe loss of Russian manpower that has resulted from losses in the first 18 months of war in Ukraine, from February 2022 to August 2023. It also includes an evaluation of Moscow's wartime recruiting and retention strategies during this period and concludes with the near-term implications for Russian military manpower.

The research reported here was completed in September 2023 and underwent security review with the sponsor and the Defense Office of Prepublication and Security Review before public release.

RAND National Security Research Division

This research was sponsored by U.S. European Command's Russia Strategic Initiative and conducted within the International Security and Defense Policy Center of the RAND National Security Research Division (NSRD), which operates the National Defense Research Institute (NDRI), a federally funded research and development center sponsored by the Office of the Secretary of Defense, the Joint Staff, the Unified Combatant Commands, the Navy, the Marine Corps, the defense agencies, and the defense intelligence enterprise.

For more information on the RAND International Security and Defense Policy Center, see www.rand.org/nsrd/isdp or contact the director (contact information provided on the webpage).

Acknowledgments

I am grateful to the U.S. European Command and the Russia Strategic Initiative for their sponsorship of this work. I thank project leaders Mark Cozad and Cortez Cooper for their support throughout the course of the research and Marek N. Posard and Andrew Monaghan for their thoughtful reviews.

I also thank Yuliya Shokh for her research on Russian military personnel accounts of the 2022 invasion. This work builds on a previously published RAND report, *Russian Military Personnel Policy and Proficiency Reforms and Trends 1991–2021*, which was also sponsored by the Russia Strategic Initiative. I thank that report's study team for their important research, which created a prewar baseline of Russian military personnel proficiency guidelines and recruiting and retention issues that is cited extensively throughout this report. That study team consists of Anika Binnendijk, Anthony Atler, John J. Drennan, Khrystyna Holynska, Katya Migacheva, Marek N. Posard, Yuliya Shokh, and me.

Summary

The research presented in this report is intended to fill a gap in analysis on what the future could hold for the Russian government's ability to recruit and retain a professional military force, given the poor treatment of its forces since the government's full-scale 2022 invasion of Ukraine. The damage to the Russian military as a result of the losses that it has sustained in Ukraine is severe and will likely lead to several challenges for recruiting and retention following the conclusion of Russia's war against Ukraine. This analysis has identified several efforts that the Russian government is pursuing to stabilize recruiting and retention. However, the heavy casualties, poor force employment, and flawed unit leadership that soldiers are experiencing first-hand will undermine these efforts.

The Russian military has sustained more casualties in 18 months of war in Ukraine than in an entire decade in Afghanistan or two campaigns in Chechnya. The effect of these casualties and the combat trauma for those who survive will have acute and lasting effects on the Russian military's ability to recruit and retain service personnel for years to come. As a result, the Russian military has been forced to take several extraordinary measures to stabilize manpower levels since its 2022 invasion of Ukraine, such as expanding financial and social benefits to would-be soldiers; lowering recruiting standards; and using private military companies, convicts, volunteer groups, and mobilization to fill its ranks. It is likely that Russia will need to continue these measures after the active phase of the war concludes as part of larger force regeneration policies.

Wartime Recruitment Efforts

The Russian government's approach to recruiting volunteers since its invasion of Ukraine has had a coherent logic. Since 2022, the government has offered competitive and tangible benefits, such as combat pay, bonuses, housing, and lifelong medical care, to stabilize recruiting and retention. Moscow is also using appeals to intangible factors, such as duty and masculinity, in its wartime recruiting campaigns. Although the wartime benefits are robust, with salaries nearly three times the national median salary, those benefits have been outweighed by multiple negative considerations, such as the breakdown of order and discipline in units, poor combat conditions, the risk of injury or death, and the spread of stories from soldiers—by word of mouth and social media—to their social networks about military life on the front. The Russian government's voluntary recruiting effort during the summer of 2022 failed to replenish losses likely because of these negative, intangible factors, which led Moscow to switch to partial mobilization of 300,000 personnel in September 2022.

After the active phase of the war in Ukraine concludes, if the Russian government continues to offer competitive tangible enlistment benefits, it might be able to recruit personnel who are enticed by economic considerations. As time goes by and memory fades, recruiting could stabilize. However, much will depend on how the conflict ends, whether the conflict is viewed as successful, and the political outcomes in Russia. The Russian government is already targeting the next generation of recruits by rapidly expanding patriotic education in schools and by inviting veterans to speak to children in their classrooms and at nationalist or militarized youth clubs in the hope that young people will be enticed to join the military in the next decade.

Military Retention

The future retention of active-duty personnel that Moscow has worked for more than a decade to professionalize is less clear. Military retention has been frozen since Russia's September 2022 mobilization decree. All personnel in Ukraine are prohibited from resigning until the end of the so-called special military operation and have had their contracts extended indefinitely. Damage to the future retention of active-duty personnel within the Ground Forces, Airborne Forces, and Special Forces is, therefore, currently unknown. However, on the basis of premobilization resignations, anecdotal evidence from the Russian frontlines, and a growing number of formally prosecuted desertions or refusals, the damage could be severe when the restrictions are lifted. In particular, the Russian military's conduct of the war in Ukraine is undermining three key prewar pillars of retention: (1) the perception of good order and discipline in the military and the perception of well-being, (2) improved service conditions within specific units and within the Russian military more broadly, and (3) broader public perceptions of military prestige.

Public Perceptions

Potentially as an offset strategy, the Russian government is trying to heavily manage patriotism and public perceptions of the war to suppress bad news, limit protests or collective bargaining, and shape public views of the military for the future. The government's efforts have kept a majority of the Russian population, at most, only passively engaged in the war and not openly critical of the operation or the troops. Efforts to manage public perceptions of the military include the following:

- framing the war in Ukraine as an existential conflict against the West to raise the stakes and increase the sense of patriotism and duty
- linking World War II iconography to the war in Ukraine and framing military personnel as liberators and heroes
- suppressing negative information about casualties, war crimes, and poor combat performance and criminalizing sensitive topics and dissent with new laws that penalize disparagement of the armed forces
- increasing military–patriotic education in schools after the full-scale invasion, potentially to shape the next generation of recruits.

Longer-Term Implications

Once the active phase of the war is over, there is another personnel crisis that is likely to emerge among Russian veterans. Many personnel will return with severe physical and mental wounds and will require lifelong benefits and financial entitlements. The Russian government is not postured to adequately cope with large numbers of casualties or the invisible wounds of posttraumatic stress disorder and other forms of mental trauma from war, despite resident expertise from previous conflicts. In Russia, there are shortfalls of facilities and trained therapists to treat an estimated 100,000 personnel, or 20–25 percent of veterans, who could need professional help after the war's end—a number that will only grow the longer the war continues.

Additionally, the Russian government's plan to expand its force size to 1.5 million personnel by the late 2020s will take place during a severe manpower deficit caused by the war in Ukraine and longer-term demographic pressures in the country. If the government is unable to double the active total of professional enlisted forces to attain this number, it could be forced to either reduce those plans or rely on a greater number of conscripts in the military, most of whom will probably be sent to the Ground Forces based on historical patterns.

Contents

Figures and Tables

Figures

Tables

CHAPTER 1

Introduction

Prior to the Russian government's 2022 full-scale invasion of Ukraine, the Russian military spent nearly 20 years trying to recruit, train, and retain a more proficient and professional military. The government allocated billions of rubles to improve military service conditions and to raise the prestige of military service through programs that included overhauling training programs; improving service conditions; modernizing the force with new or improved equipment; instituting measures to reduce corruption, hazing, and criminality; and offering more-attractive incentives, such as competitive wages, housing, and other social benefits, to officers and professional enlisted personnel.[1]

Russian civilian and military leaders believed that these efforts increased military proficiency and improved the prestige of military service. On the basis of some metrics, this belief was not groundless. In the years prior the 2022 invasion, the Russian military was able—for the first time in its history—to count more professional enlisted personnel in its ranks than

---

[1] P. Bruntalsky [П. Брунтальский], "The Soldier Has a Day Off . . . Saturday and Sunday" ["У солдата выходной . . . Суббота и воскресенье"], *Military Industrial Courier* [Военно-промышленный курьер], No. 20, 2010; Keith Crane, Olga Oliker, and Brian Nichiporuk, *Trends in Russia's Armed Forces: An Overview of Budgets and Capabilities*, RAND Corporation, RR-2573-A, 2019; Yuri Gavrilov [Гаврилов, Юрий], "Spring Recruitment into the Army Has Begun. 135 Thousand People Will Become Soldiers" ["Начался весенний набор в армию. Солдатами станут 135 тысяч человек"], *Rossiyskaya Gazeta* [Российской газеты], March 31, 2019; Ministry of Defense of the Russian Federation [Министерство обороны Российской Федерации], "Social Benefits Package of the Contract Service Member" ["Социальный пакет военнослужащего-контрактника"], undated-e; Konstantin Raschepkin [Константин Ращепкин] and Viktor Pyakov [Виктор Пьяков], "The Path to Professionalism" ["Путь в профессионалы"], *On Duty* [На боевом посту], Vols. 69–70, 2008.

conscripts.[2] It also conducted two campaigns abroad (in Ukraine in 2014 and in Syria in 2015) that met objectives without major operational failings. The Russian military met many of its benchmarks for force modernization, personnel recruiting, and retention by 2020, as it sought to create a more modern military prepared for modern challenges. However, problems still lurked: Russia clamped down on public discussion of military topics, and information about military readiness was either withheld or partially discussed during carefully managed press conferences. Regardless, official statistics suggested that, at the war's start, personnel recruiting had stagnated or that Russian combat units were understrength. The Russian military's personnel problems ran deep and would be fully exposed on the battlefield.

During the start of its invasion of Ukraine, the Russian government committed an estimated 190,000 troops to a multi-axis attack on northern, eastern, and southern Ukraine. Because of fierce Ukrainian resistance that has been supported by weapons and intelligence from the West, Russia has been unable to achieve its prewar strategic goals, and wartime losses have been catastrophic for the Russian military. After 18 months of war, parts of the Russian military are severely damaged from extensive casualties and equipment losses. Russian casualties are estimated at 200,000 to 300,000 as of summer 2023 by various Ukrainian, Western government, and media

---

[2]   By 2016, the Russian government claimed that, for the first time, at all noncommissioned officer (NCO) positions were filled by contract personnel. Before 2022, recruiting priorities were for certain specialties, such as pilots, test pilots, and engineers. Prior RAND Corporation research analysis of the Ministry of Defense's (MOD's) recruiting priorities revealed a preference from 2013 to 2020 for all-contract units for submarine crews, special brigade combat units, Airborne Forces (VDV), marine battalions, artillery reconnaissance, technical personnel, drivers, combat unit maintenance personnel, and operators of complex and expensive weapons and equipment (Ministry of Defense of the Russian Federation [Министерство обороны Российской Федерации], "Action Plan 2013–2020: Improving the Quality of Troop Training" ["План деятельности на 2013–2020 гг: повышение качества подготовки войск"], undated-a; Ministry of Defense of the Russian Federation [Министерство обороны Российской Федерации], "Testimony of the Minister of Defense of the Russian Federation General of the Army Sergei Shoigu at the Russian Defense Ministry Board Session" ["Выступление Министра обороны Российской Федерации генерала армии С.К. Шойгу на расширенном заседании Коллегии Миногороны России"], December 22, 2016).

sources.[3] Of those casualties, an estimated 47,000 to 60,000 Russian personnel have been killed in action; official information from Moscow almost certainly undercounts those deaths (around 6,000). Russian casualties from 18 months of war now exceed the number of casualties from a decade of war in Afghanistan or two campaigns in Chechnya in the 1990s.[4] Already by September 2022, personnel losses were so severe that the Kremlin was forced to order a partial mobilization of 300,000 people.[5]

The images and stories from occupied Ukraine paint a bleak picture of indifference and cruelty to Russian military personnel by their own command while at war. As of fall 2023, Russia's forces in occupied Ukraine are made up of the remnants of its exhausted professional enlisted forces, mobilized soldiers with highly variable training, and private military companies (PMCs). Instances of physical and emotional abuse from Russian military personnel against each other, and particularly from commanders, have found their way onto Russian social media and into independent Russian media abroad, as have videos from the soldiers and their families detailing poor conditions and appealing for help.[6] The future of Russia's professional military forces hangs in the balance. How will the Russian

---

[3] Helene Cooper, Thomas Gibbons-Neff, Eric Schmitt, and Julian E. Barnes, "Troop Deaths and Injuries in Ukraine War Near 500,000, U.S. Officials Say," *New York Times*, August 18, 2023; Ministry of Defence [@DefenceHQ], "INTELLIGENCE UPDATE: Russia retains a significant military presence that can conduct an invasion without further warning," post on the X platform, February 17, 2022; George Wright, "Ukraine War: More Than 20,000 Russian Troops Killed Since December, U.S. Says," BBC News, May 1, 2023.

[4] Seth G. Jones, Riley McCabe, and Alexander Palmer, *Ukrainian Innovation in a War of Attrition*, Center for Strategic and International Studies, February 27, 2023; Wright, 2023.

[5] "Russia Calls Up 300,000 Reservists, Says 6,000 Soldiers Killed in Ukraine," Reuters, September 21, 2022.

[6] "Draftees from Irkutsk Appeal to Putin for Help: 'Command Told Us Directly That We Are Expendable,'" Meduza, February 26, 2023; WarTranslated (Dmitri) [@wartranslated], "Another group of Russian mobiks lost in Ukraine," post on the X platform, February 18, 2023a; WarTranslated (Dmitri) [@wartranslated], "Russian women appeal to Putin for assistance with their mobilised men—in this new video . . . ," May 21, 2023b.

military recruit and retain a professional force after all that has transpired since invading Ukraine in 2022?

This report seeks to fill a gap in analysis on what the future could hold for the Russian government's ability to recruit and retain a professional military force, given the poor treatment of its forces since the government's full-scale invasion of Ukraine. This report seeks to answer the following questions:

- How is the Russian government trying to stabilize its available wartime personnel through the use of recruiting and retention policies?
- How will military recruiting for Russian officers and enlisted professional be affected as a result of the 2022 war in Ukraine?
- What are the implications for Russian military retention once the active phase of the war in Ukraine has concluded?
- What does the future hold for Russian military personnel polices as a result of the war in Ukraine?

Background

RAND researchers have previously examined how the Russian military from 1991 through 2021 developed and implemented personnel policies to develop a professional force. The research for that report, *Russian Military Personnel Policy and Proficiency: Reforms and Trends, 1991–2021*, was co-led by Anika Binnendijk and me and focused on how the Russian military attempted to reform, recruit, and retain a more proficient professional military force over 30 years.[7] That research ended in 2021, prior to Russia's 2022 full-scale invasion of Ukraine. The report used information from several sources, such as Russian government-commissioned studies and military personnel polls, that were designed to understand solider motivations to join and remain in service. That information was used in conjunction with other Russian-language sources to understand various aspects of Russian military life.

---

[7] Anika Binnendijk, Dara Massicot, Anthony Atler, John J. Drennan, Khrystyna Holynska, Katya Migacheva, Marek N. Posard, and Yuliya Shokh, *Russian Military Personnel Policy and Proficiency: Reforms and Trends, 1991–2021*, RAND Corporation, RR-A1233-6, 2023.

This report uses a prewar baseline of Russian military proficiency, recruiting, and retention policies described in the earlier RAND report by Binnendijk and colleagues and evaluates the evidence and policy choices that have been made since Russia's February 2022 invasion of Ukraine.

Sources and Methods

There are many limitations on the amount of available open-source information from Russia about the Russian military, particularly since the implementation of new laws that increase penalties for discussing certain defense topics.[8] This process of limiting publicly available information about the military accelerated after the war began in 2022, which has made a wide swath of military topics off-limits in public discourse. The legal penalties for discussing topics related to the war have been strengthened and Russian law has criminalized unflattering portrayals of the war as "disparaging to the armed services."[9] These laws have led to self-censorship for many Russian media outlets and outright bans for independent media sources, and many of the latter have now relocated abroad.

For this report, new sources of information (since 2022) are used, which provide fresh insights about Russian military personnel issues that were not previously available. This information came from a variety of sources that could be cross-checked and corroborated, such as Ukrainian government and media sources, Western government and media sources, social media, and Russian opposition media (exiled abroad). These sources provide unique looks inside Russian military units that had not been known in such detail previously. Furthermore, a growing body of accounts from Russian service personnel (e.g., intercepted phone calls released by Ukrainian government sources that were assumed to be authentic but could not be inde-

---

[8] "Russian FSB Approves New List of Information That Could Pose National Security Threat," Meduza, October 1, 2021.

[9] In October 2021, the Federal Security Service's (FSB's) new list of information that "could be used to threaten the security of the Russian Federation" or that could cause a Russian entity or citizen to be considered a "foreign agent" ("Russian FSB Approves New List," 2021).

pendently verified), Russian defectors, recovered Russian military orders and planning documents in Ukraine, and extensive media interviews with Ukrainian Armed Forces (UAF) personnel provide a rich source of new information. This report avoids using information that was obtained from Russian or Ukrainian prisoner of war testimonies or from interrogations and also avoids using information from unauthorized disclosures of classified information.

The Russian government uses the term *special military operation* (SMO) to describe its full-scale invasion of Ukraine, largely for domestic purposes to downplay and to obfuscate its actions. This report does not use that term unless needed, for example, to refer to specific Russian legislation, an official decree, or a quotation. This report instead uses the term *full-scale invasion* to describe Russia's initial operations to occupy Ukraine in February 2022, and the term *war* to describe Russia's actions since that time. This report acknowledges that Russia's limited invasion of Ukraine began with the illegal annexation of Crimea and the partial occupation of Ukraine's Luhansk and Donetsk regions in 2014. The scope of this research begins in 2022 and extends through September 2023.

Structure of This Report

This report is structured as follows. Chapter 1 presents an outline of the research and a baseline understanding of prewar Russian military personnel policies that contributed to the recruiting and retention of a professional force. I define the professional force as encompassing Russian officers, professional enlisted (also known as contract service personnel or *contractniki* in Russian), and professional reservists. I do not study conscripts in depth for this research, as conscripts are not currently deployed to occupied Ukraine.[10] In Chapter 2, I discuss the effects of the war in Ukraine on Russian military manpower. In Chapter 3, I discuss wartime recruiting and retention policies and how they could be affected after wartime restrictions

---

[10] Kevin Ryan, "Is the Russian Military Running Out of Soldiers?" Harvard Kennedy School Belfer Center for Science and International Affairs, Russia Matters, March 28, 2022.

are lifted and personnel are allowed to leave service.[11] The report concludes in Chapter 4 with findings and implications for Russian military personnel issues after the active phase of the war ends. I note that the implications for military manpower and future recruiting and retention will be contingent on how the war ends, the status of forces at that time, whether the war is viewed as a success or failure by the Russian population, and the status of the political system and economy in Russia.

Russian Personnel Reforms 1991–2021: A Work in Progress Toward a More Professional Force

As previous RAND research on Russian military personnel proficiency, recruiting, and retention noted, the Russian military devoted considerable resources to reforming its personnel policies over a 30-year period, beginning in 1991.[12] The military's problems in these realms were numerous and, for a brief period in the 2000s to the early 2010s, the problems were discussed openly and relatively frankly by parts of the government, the media, and nongovernmental organizations (NGOs). In earlier RAND analysis, Russian military personnel problems were summarized as follows:

- understrength (defined as when a unit's total manpower is below authorized billets or when billets are unfilled or empty) and low readiness in many units
- problems with training quality and a lack of funds
- low military prestige and popular support
- hazing
- high rates of draft evasion
- high rates of health problems and deferments

---

[11] At the time of writing, the Russian authorities have suspended the ability for any personnel to voluntarily leave the military, starting in September 2022, unless they are conscripts that are at the end of their 12-month service term, are at retirement age, are injured, or are imprisoned. This condition will continue until the period of "partial mobilization" is declared over (Zoya Sheftalovich, "Full Text of Putin's Mobilization Decree—Translated," Politico, September 21, 2022).

[12] Binnendijk et al., 2023.

- disillusionment among active-duty personnel
- wage issues
- criminality and corruption
- desertion.[13]

Table 1.1 is adapted from Binnendijk et al. (2023) and summarizes these issues and whether they affected proficiency, recruiting, and retention prior to the war in Ukraine. There have been multiple reform efforts in the Russian military; some efforts ended in failure because they were underfunded, poorly implemented, or simply misconceived. Nonetheless, each failure was a learning event and the MOD would make a renewed attempt using some of those lessons.

Ultimately, the most-lasting changes from between 1991 and 2021 were the 2009-era "New Look" reforms instituted under General Nikolay Makarov and Defense Minister Anatoly Serdyukov, which followed the lackluster display of Russian capabilities during Russia's five-day war against Georgia in 2008. A necessary element for this rapid reformation to work from 2009 to 2012 was the candor that was permitted within the military, and in Russian society more broadly, about the state of military affairs. These reforms were a comprehensive attempt to modernize the military with better equipment and professional, proficient forces. Russian military personnel policies were centered on the following initiatives, which lasted through 2021:

- **increasing benefits** in the form of better wages, housing, mortgage assistance, and health benefits
- **humanizing the service** for personnel and families by changing conscription to 12 months, granting more access to conscripts, and allowing conscripts to serve near their homes; modifying the contract

---

[13] Bettina Renz, *Russia's Military Revival*, Polity Press, 2018, p. 53; Jason P. Gresh, "The Realities of Russian Military Conscription," *Journal of Slavic Military Studies*, Vol. 24, No. 2, 2011, p. 189; Dale R. Herspring, "Undermining Combat Readiness in the Russian Military, 1992–2005," *Armed Forces & Society*, Vol. 32, No. 4, July 2006, pp. 520–521; Carolina Vendil Pallin, *Russian Military Reform: A Failed Exercise in Defence Decision Making*, Routledge, 2009, pp. 107–108.

TABLE 1.1

Summary of Military Personnel Issues from 1991 to 2021 Reforms and Recent Trends

Problem	Contributing Factors	Proficiency Issue	Recruitment Issue	Retention Issue	Trends Prior to 2021
Understrength and low readiness in units	• Inherited legacy Soviet force structure • Insufficient staffing, budget, and justification	X	X	X	Improved manpower levels and readiness metrics
Low-quality training and a lack of funds	• Poor quality, outdated, and irregular training created by force consolidation and a poor economy	X			Investments and reforms yielding improved frequent training and performance standards
Low military prestige and popular support	• Endemic problems and social changes led to a decrease in prestige and a decline in popular support for military service		X	X	Stronger popular support for the military and enhanced prestige because of perceptions of success in conflicts pre-2021
Hazing and other poor service conditions	• Violent hazing or the extortion of conscripts and junior officers • Bad conditions on the base • Few incentives to join or stay in the military	X	X	X	A reduction in hazing, court cases, and survey data suggesting that cases persisted but at lower levels
Draft evasion	• Poor conditions and hazing meant families were desperate to keep male family members from serving		X		Lower rates of draft evasion

Table 1.1-Continued

Problem	Contributing Factors	Proficiency Issue	Recruitment Issue	Retention Issue	Trends Prior to 2021
Health problems and personnel deferments	• Poor physical and mental health of the eligible male Russian population made recruitment more difficult and costly		X		Remained problematic in terms of the physical and mental health of Russian youth
Military disillusionment	• Deep-seated post-Soviet morale crisis within military and society more broadly	X	X	X	Renewed policy emphasis on the moral–psychological dimensions of readiness
Wage issues	• Financial problems led to arrears and poor pay compared with other sectors		X	X	Improved compensation, particularly for highly valued roles
Criminality and corruption	• Crime within units • Graft • Siphoning of funds • Bribes	X	X	X	Some improvement, yet remained problematic; good order and discipline were identified as a recruitment factor
Desertion	• Poor service conditions led some service members to desert			X	Lower rates of peacetime desertion

SOURCE: Adapted from Binnendijk et al., 2023.

enlistment process to give conscripts a choice in where they serve and in career paths; creating new, on-base amenities and social supports

- **reforming command styles** by teaching officers not to treat professional enlisted personnel as more experienced conscripts but as professionals who had chosen to serve

- **regaining social trust and prestige** for the military with new equipment; more-realistic training and busier days to reduce opportunities for hazing; anticorruption measures, including electronic wages to curb wage siphoning and rotating officials at local military commissariats to break up corruption networks; new military-patriotic organizations for students; and the use of successful military operations as recruiting and retention tools. According to Levada-Center polling, the military was, as of 2021, the most trusted and approved institution among Russians, including youth.[14]

Previous RAND analysis studied how the Russian military and government used a mixture of *tangible benefits* and *intangible benefits* to develop, recruit, and retain personnel. For that analysis, the study team included a review of Western and Russian scholarship on factors that contribute to the recruitment of a volunteer force. Those motivations can be framed by two categories: *occupational benefits* or tangible benefits, including housing, compensation, health care, social benefits (e.g., prioritization for higher education), family benefits (e.g., spousal opportunities), and childcare subsidies; and *institutional benefits* or intangible benefits, such as norms or codes of service, order and discipline, patriotism (pride in service and patriotic duty), reduced stigma, and an increase in the prestige of serving in the armed forces.[15] According to this previous RAND study, intangible benefits, such as prestige and reduced stigma associated with military service, appear to play a less significant role in recruitment and retention in

---

[14] "Military Conscription," Levada-Center, July 13, 2021.

[15] Beth J. Asch, *Setting Military Compensation to Support Recruitment, Retention, and Performance*, RAND Corporation, RR-3197-A, 2019; Charles C. Moskos, Jr., "From Institution to Occupation: Trends in Military Organization," *Armed Forces & Society*, Vol. 4, No. 1, Fall 1977; Charles C. Moskos, "Institutional/Occupational Trends in Armed Forces: An Update," *Armed Forces & Society*, Vol. 12, No. 3, Spring 1986.

Russia—particularly for contract personnel—than tangible benefits, such as wages, although intangible factors did contribute.[16]

The results of Russia's personnel reforms were mixed prior to the 2022 invasion according to previous RAND analysis. On the one hand, Russia allocated significant funds and attention to many of these problem areas.[17] Russia's defense leadership prioritized the professionalization of the Russian military through policy and budgetary initiatives in tandem with other modernization investments in weapons and equipment. Demonstrable progress was made in many metrics in terms of recruiting, retention, and proficiency when 2009 (reform start) is used as a baseline.

On the other hand, these revisions to personnel policies addressed—but did not resolve—several of the perennial problems of Russian military culture that had hampered the military's effectiveness. Graft and embezzlement continued and were only occasionally punished in the legal system as part of anticorruption measures; the overall rates of corruption did not steadily decline.[18] Hazing problems or breakdowns in unit discipline still occurred but with a decline in numbers. As found in the previous RAND study, individual soldier proficiency across the Russian military was highly varied, a deficit that came into sharp focus during combat operations against Ukraine in 2022. The previous study also found a trust deficit within the Russian military: Senior commanders might not fully trust their personnel, even as more personnel served under contract.[19] It was also observed that since 2019, the Russian government accelerated efforts to improve the loyalty of all service members by promoting lessons of military history and patriotic values at all echelons.[20] Through revisions to programs, policies, and training since the 2010s, Russian military leaders aimed to create a force that could demonstrate high technical competence in combat.

---

[16] Binnendijk et al., 2023.

[17] Binnendijk et al., 2023.

[18] Anna Svetlova [Анна Светлова], "There Is Less Hazing and More Corruption in the Russian Armed Forces" ["В российской армии стало меньше дедовщины и больше коррупции"], Gazeta.ru [Газета.Ру], March 10, 2021.

[19] Binnendijk et al., 2023.

[20] Binnendijk et al., 2023.

Prewar Recruiting Policies and Key Factors

As noted, earlier RAND analysis included a review of Western and Russian scholarship on factors that contribute to the recruitment of a volunteer force. Prior to the 2022 invasion, contract service personnel were offered several types of benefits during the recruitment process. Tangible benefits included base pay, which Russia has tried to keep nationally competitive since the 2010s; bonuses that varied according to specialty, clearance status, and service location; housing support (on-base housing or mortgage assistance for an apartment); better service conditions and on-base amenities; and childcare subsidies and other social supports for family members. Wages and housing assistance in particular were important recruiting tools.[21] In addition, motivations for joining the military varied by region and socioeconomic status. Urbanites tended to view military service in pragmatic terms, for the wages, housing, and other benefits. Those in rural areas tended to self-report intangibles, such as job stability, prestige or social standing, and the means for geographic mobility, as motivation for joining the military.[22]

Russia's prewar recruiting policy was centered on offering competitive benefits while raising military prestige and patriotism. Recruiting enticements for officers and professional enlisted personnel before 2022 included a combination of tangible benefits (increases to wages and social benefits, the promise of better service conditions) and intangible benefits (a higher degree of professionalism and the prestige of military service). At the same time, military–patriotic efforts targeting preconscription-age youth, and Russian society more broadly, grew significantly. The goal of these pro-

---

[21] In 2014, a poll of service personnel conducted by the Sociological Center for the Russian Armed Forces noted that 55 percent of contract personnel said that pay and benefits were their primary reason for enlisting (Nadja Douglas, "Civil–Military Relations in Russia: Conscript vs. Contract Army, or How Ideas Prevail Against Functional Demands," *Journal of Slavic Military Studies*, Vol. 27, No. 4, 2014).

[22] Ludmila Vladislavovna Klimenko [Людмила Владиславовна Клименко] and Oksana Yurievna Posukhova [Оксана Юрьевна Посухова], "Russian Military Personnel Under Institutional Reforms: Professional Attitudes and Identity" ["Российские военнослужащие в условиях институциональных реформ: профессиональные установки и идентичность"], *Journal of Institutional Studies* [*Журнал Институциональных Исследований*], Vol. 10, No. 2, June 2018.

grams and increased presence via movies or television specials was designed to keep the Russian military visible, familiar, and accessible to Russian society, along with the indirect benefit of aiding recruitment.

Several metrics suggest that these efforts paid off. Rates of draft evasion declined, and Russia's official contract service personnel numbers remained stable (but still anywhere from 5–9 percent short of MOD benchmarks) and were finally more numerous than conscripts.[23] As of 2021, the Russian military was the most highly trusted institution according to NGO polls, consistent with several years of similar polling results.[24]

However, there were still unresolved issues with respect to recruiting prior to the full-scale invasion of Ukraine. A harsh military culture within some units, hazing, inadequate housing in some areas, and the poor physical and mental health of preconscription youth were all challenges to creating the professional force Russia wanted.[25] These issues were not significant enough to affect the conduct of the Russian military's 2014 invasion of Ukraine or its operations in Syria because those campaigns were much smaller, designed with limited objectives, and did not strain available personnel in contrast with Moscow's 2022 invasion of Ukraine.

Prewar Retention Policies and Key Contributing Factors

The research co-led by Binnendijk and me found that for retention, the tangible benefits of military service (such as wages, healthcare, and housing) were important motivators for remaining in the military, although intangible benefits (such as prestige or patriotism) played a role as well. That research found that up until 2022, the Russian military used a mixture of intangible or *institutional benefits* (e.g., maintaining good order and discipline, promoting a sense of patriotism, and managing public perceptions of the military to promote prestige and reduce stigma) and tangible or *occu-*

---

[23] The last publicly available figure for the total number of professional contract service personnel is 405,000, issued in 2020 by the Russian military ("There Will Be Half a Million Contract Soldiers in the Russian Army" ["В российской армии будет полмиллиона контрактников"], Interfax [Интерфакс], December 18, 2020).

[24] Binnendijk et al., 2023.

[25] Binnendijk et al., 2023.

pational benefits (e.g., increasing the compensation of contract personnel, improving the well-being of their families, and creating educational and professional development opportunities) to encourage retention. Intangible benefits, such as command climate and service conditions, were important factors for military personnel to remain in service.

In the previous study, as in this one, *military retention* is defined in the following ways:

- *Retention in active-duty service*: Contract renewals and retention in active-duty service are offered to enlisted personnel and officers. At end of the first contract, contractniki are offered another contract or to enter specially designed military education programs to convert to an officer.
- *Retention in the strategic reserves or professional reserves*: This includes reserves such as the Special Combat Army Reserve (Boevoy Armeyskiy Rezerv Strany or BARS). Conscripts and contract service personnel who complete their service terms are automatically entered into the strategic reserves. Minister of Defense Sergei Shoigu has claimed that the strategic reserves consist of 25 million reservists.[26]
- *Retention within the Russian government*: There is a program that facilitates transfer to other parts of the government, such as the intelligence, security, or civil services.[27]
- *Retention into fully or partially funded state-sponsored PMCs*: This initiative includes the Wagner Group or new PMCs created since 2022 to fight in Ukraine.

Previous RAND research found that intangible benefits were important for Russian military personnel retention, but they did not offset the need for tangible benefits.[28] Housing benefits and mortgage assistance were noted

---

[26] "Russia Calls Up 300,000 Reservists," 2022.

[27] "Conscripts Were Offered Permission to Conclude a Contract with the FSB" ["Военнослужащим-срочникам предложили разрешать заключать контракт с ФСБ"], RIA News [РИА Новости], November 1, 2021.

[28] By 2014, 55 percent of polled respondents noted that wages were the top draw to military service, while 18 percent believed it was a matter of civic duty (Binnendijk et al.,

as a major component of retention in service personnel surveys conducted by the government, along with family well-being, which tended to be influenced by comfortable and safe housing, job opportunities for spouses, and access to education and childcare.[29] The Russian MOD and various sociological organizations found that different tangible benefits appealed to personnel according to their age and social status.[30] Those efforts began to pay off prewar, as the quality of life and housing satisfaction began to rise. There were notable variations by region and by respondent age, however, suggesting a systemic lack of oversight or funds to realize those policy programs.[31]

Increasing wages was also an important retention factor and a key priority for the MOD prewar. In the 1990s, low wages kept many officers in poverty, which proved to be destructive to retention and to prestige more broadly for the military as a profession. According to the MOD's Sociology Center, in the late 1990s, 25 percent of officers and 50 percent of enlisted families had incomes below the poverty line.[32] By 2008, around 30 percent of officers who held the rank of major and below and professional enlisted were earning wages at or below the poverty line according to the Minis-

---

2023; Douglas, 2014).

[29] Binnendijk et al., 2023.

[30] For example, with housing, 30 percent of Russian contract personnel get married during their first contract. After five years of service, this number grows to 90 percent according to Russian estimates from 2013. As a result, by 2008, the MOD prioritized the construction of family housing, mortgage assistance for off-base housing, and social supports, such as on-base amenities, better schools, and programs for spousal employment (Dmitriy Makarov [Дмитрий Макаров], "Contract Signed? [Есть контракт]," *Flag of the Motherland* [*Флаг родины*], July 9, 2013, p. 73).

[31] RAND researchers noted that in the region around Moscow, one of the most sought-after locations, satisfaction increased in the Air Force from 25 percent in 2005 to 66 percent in 2016 on average. However, that satisfaction dropped as airman age and time in service increased. Housing dissatisfaction was higher outside Moscow; for example, in Nizhny Novgorod, only 8 percent said their housing was comfortable and in the Central Military District, the largest military district in Russia, just 32 percent expressed satisfaction.

[32] Ministry of Defense of the Russian Federation [Министерство обороны Российской Федерации], "Russian Army: Social Problems and Ways to Solve Them" ["Российская армия: социальные проблемы и способы их решения"], undated-d.

try of Health and Social Development.[33] Increasing wages was a priority for the Kremlin, and several federal programs were devoted to keeping wages at competitive levels.[34] Wages and bonuses were complicated and highly variable and were calculated according to location, specialty, and retention requirements. In general, the Russian government has made resources available to keep military salaries at a competitive level, particularly for entry- to mid-level positions, compared with civilian indexing.

Other tangible benefits designed to increase retention rates that were implemented in prior to the February 2022 invasion included a 40-hour workweek, free health care for life, 45 days of vacation (including 15 days for train travel), 80–90 percent of childcare paid by the state, and priority placement in civilian daycare centers near bases.[35] Many personnel also received a contract completion bonus. Military personnel had the right to retirement housing after a certain number of years of service and some choice in the location. They also received 50 percent of their pay as a retirement pension and benefits for serving in hardship locations (austere or remote bases), such as bonuses and counting time served at those facilities as double toward service time.[36]

Intangible or Institutional Benefits and Retention

Previous RAND analysis found that three clusters of intangible factors affect retention and are important to consider in light of the war in Ukraine.[37] These clusters are (1) the perception of good order and discipline and perceptions of well-being, (2) service conditions within specific units and more broadly within the Russian military, and (3) patriotism and broader public perceptions of Russian military service. Two of these factors are at serious risk as a result of Russian military performance and the command climate within occupied Ukraine, and the Russian government is attempting to heavily manage the third, public perceptions. As I discuss in subsequent

---

[33] Douglas, 2014.

[34] Douglas, 2014.

[35] Binnendijk et al., 2023.

[36] Binnendijk et al., 2023.

[37] Binnendijk et al., 2023.

chapters, all three of these factors are lagging and the authorities are allocating resources to improve them.

Order and Discipline

Perceptions of good order and discipline affect individual decisions to continue with military service. As prior RAND researchers noted, hazing, bullying, and harassment are widely studied problems in Russian military literature related to good order and discipline.[38] Hazing also affects job satisfaction and other factors that serve as a basis for retention for professional enlisted personnel and officers. Many attempts were made to change the structural factors that contributed to the lack of discipline or order within units, and those efforts reduced, but did not eradicate, some of the more violent issues. Furthermore, Russian crackdowns on NGOs and independent media (by branding them as foreign agents or as undesirable organizations) limited the types of information that were available about what was happening inside the majority of Russian units.

In the years prior to the full-scale invasion, the Russian military began to backtrack on some of the measures to improve service conditions and humanize the service. For example, military leadership disallowed conscripts having their own smartphones in 2021, after they were permitted in the early 2010s to communicate with family and friends.[39] One poll in 2020 revealed that 55 percent of respondents said that they had experienced some type of hazing in the military in the past six years.[40] Just one year prior, Minister of Defense Shoigu claimed that hazing (*dedovshchina*) had mostly been eliminated. Shoigu maintained that as long as crime rates were below

[38] A. N. Dyachenko [А. Н. Дяченко] and V. N. Kozlov [В. Н. Козлов], "Hazing in the Russian Army as a Factor of Evasion from Military Service" ["Неуставные отношения в Российской армии как фактор уклонения от военной службы"], *Oboznik* [*Обозник*], October 2, 2018.

[39] "The General Staff Explained How the Ban on Smartphones for Conscripts Works" ["В Генштабе объяснили, как работает запрет на смартфоны для призывников"], RBC [РБК], March 31, 2021.

[40] Katya Arenina [Катя Аренина], "'I Would Then Be Missing in Action': How and Why Contract Soldiers Flee the Russian Army" ["'Был бы потом без вести пропавшим': Как и почему контрактники бегут из российской армии"], Important Stories [Важные истории], October 29, 2020.

average, progress could be claimed; yet, for most of his tenure, the MOD has not released crime statistics, only percentages of change.[41]

Service Conditions

Improving the command climate within units was recognized as an important retention tool to retain qualified professionals. In Western and Russian scholarship, unit cohesion, leadership, and morale are known and important intangible factors that affect retention rates.[42] The goal was to treat professional enlisted personnel with respect because they were the ones who had chosen a life of military service and should not be treated as more experienced conscripts. However, changing the command climate within individual units proved to be hard to accomplish during the more than ten years between the 2009 New Look reforms and the Russian government's full-scale invasion of Ukraine. In the decade prior to the war, surveys of service personnel conducted by the military and various sociological organizations about command issues and discipline to correlate factors with retention suggest that military leadership had at least some understanding that problems remained.[43] It is not clear whether the MOD responded to these negative polling results, such as by relieving commanders or instituting more checks or oversight. Base cleanliness and construction projects also lagged in some areas, which led to substandard conditions, such as a lack of dividers between toilet stalls or sinks that did not function.[44] This suggests that these problems continued to fester under the surface, despite pronounce-

---

[41] Ministry of Defense of the Russian Federation [Министерство обороны Российской Федерации], "On the Results of Performance of the Ministry of Defense of the Russian Federation in 2016" ["Итоги деятельности Министерства обороны Российской Федерации в 2016 году"], undated-c.

[42] N. A. Ermolov [Н. А. Ермолов] and E. N. Karlova [Е. Н. Карлова], "Motivation for Military Service as a Subject of Theoretical and Empirical Research in Military Sociology" ["Мотивация к военной службе как предмет теоретических и эмпирических исследований в военной социологии"], *Academy* [*Академия*], Vol. 1, No. 28, 2018.

[43] Binnendijk et al., 2023.

[44] Pavel Vasilyev, "Across the Minefields. Eight Mobilised Russian Soldiers Fled the War Zone in Ukraine and Were Accused of Desertion," Mediazona, February 5, 2023.

ments from military leadership in Moscow that personnel problems were at low levels.[45]

Patriotism, Perceptions, and Retention

The third cluster of intangible benefits that contribute to retention in Russia involves issues of patriotism and broader public perceptions of Russian military service. Public perception of the military is an important retention tool according to previous RAND analysis.[46] Patriotism and belief that their work was important were important factors in service personnel motivation, but these factors did not outrank material benefits, such as wages and living conditions, according to several studies led by various Russian organizations from the 2000s to 2019.[47] The MOD has devoted resources to raising public perceptions of the military as prestigious prior to the 2022 invasion of Ukraine. Studies of officers and enlisted personnel from different regions of the country found that 60–69 percent of respondents claimed that perceptions of military prestige had increased from 2012 to 2017. Interestingly, when asked to look to the future, a smaller percentage of the same respondents thought that prestige would continue to increase in the next five years: just 38–40 percent.[48] The reasons those respondents did not believe that Russian military prestige would continue to improve are not precisely

---

[45] For example, the MOD conducted polling on service conditions, hazing, and command climate throughout the 2010s to understand the scope of the issues. Eastern Military District personnel who did not renew their contracts were surveyed in 2017 about why they left: overwork, remoteness, and poor treatment by commanders were top replies.

[46] Binnendijk et al., 2023.

[47] Yu. G. Bychenko [Ю. Г. Быченко] and T. M. Balandina [Т. М. Баландина], "Development of the Professional Potential of Military Personnel Who Entered Military Service Under a Contract" ["Развитие профессионального потенциала военнослужащих, поступивших на военную службу по контракту"], *Bulletin of Nizhny Novgorod University* [*Вестник Нижегородского университета*], Vol. 4, No. 56, 2019; Douglas, 2014; R. R. Kurbanov [Р. Р. Курбанов], "Monetary Benefit of the Contemporary Military Service Member" ["Денежное довольствие современного военнослужащего"], *Meridian* [*Меридиан*], Vol. 18, 2020, p. 27; Valentina Pavlova [Валентина Павлова], "Motivation of Volunteers for Contract Military Service" ["Мотивация добровольцев на военную службу по контракту"], *Russian Military Review* [*Российское военное обозрение*], Vol. 11, No. 46, November 2007.

[48] Binnendijk et al., 2023.

known; the authors of the Russian study ascribed economic anxieties stemming from economic troubles elsewhere in Russia at the time.

Patriotism and the moral–psychological readiness of personnel are factors that contribute to combat readiness at the individual and unit levels in Russian military thought.[49] Two strategists of Russian military thought, S. V. Goncharov and B. B. Ostroverkhiy, refer to previous Russian military psychologists from the 20th century who believed that the Imperial Russian Army collapsed during World War I because "no enthusiasm in the army is possible when there is no enthusiasm in the Fatherland."[50] Therefore, in their view as of 2015, a critical aspect of military readiness at the individual and unit levels should be the return of psychological and patriotic education to the units in a significant way. Russia recreated the Political–Military Directorate in 2019 to undertake this work.

RAND researchers previously noted that since 2018, the MOD has made a series of modifications to its efforts to increase patriotism among service personnel and society writ large, which coincided with the reestablishment of the Political–Military Directorate in 2019. This directorate is charged with multiple tasks, such as instilling patriotism, increasing awareness among personnel of the role that they play in defending Russia and its values, and implementing the rules of war and obligations under international law in war. In the Soviet Union, political officers were referred to as *zampolit* (sometimes derisively) and were charged with ensuring compliance with communism and Soviet Communist Party values. Political officers are sometimes still referred to as *zampolit* among the rank and file and have less of a defined political ideology to promote, but they are still responsible for framing the war in Ukraine for Russian service personnel.

---

[49] Russian strategists write often about the *sociopolitical situation*, a set of economic, social, political, demographic, and environmental factors that affect the moral, political, and psychological state of military personnel (S. V. Goncharov [С. В. Гончаров] and B. B. Ostroverkhiy [В. В. Островерхий], "Assessment and Accounting by the Commander of a Formation (Military Unit) of the Socio-Political Situation in the Area of Upcoming Hostilities" ["Оценка И Учет Командиром Соединения (Воинской Части) Социально-Политической Обстановки В Районе Предстоящих Боевых Действий"], *Military Thought* [*Военная мысль*], No. 8, August 2021).

[50] Goncharov and Ostroverkhiy, 2021, p. 100.

In 2021, Russian strategists Goncharov and Ostroverkhiy proposed measuring the patriotic mood of individual personnel in the military or among the Russian population more broadly by ranking certain personal characteristics from 1 to 4 based on observations (the results can be found in Table 1.2). A score of 1 suggests that an individual or group is actively opposed to an armed conflict, which could lead to protests or resistance to orders, and a score of 4 is considered an individual or group that is fully invested in a total or "peoples" war.[51] The strategists argued that proper political work can change negative scores (1 or 2) to a 3 or 4 to raise patriotism and the moral–psychological readiness of soldiers.

TABLE 1.2

Measuring Views on the Nature of an Armed Conflict

Social-Political Factor Score	Score Definition and Indicators
1	• Extremely negative public opinion in relation to the participation of their side in the armed conflict • Numerous mass protests • Opposition statements by authoritative politicians • An open expression of distrust in the country's leadership
2	• Hidden dissatisfaction with the armed conflict • The absence of signs of general antagonism toward the enemy • A tolerant attitude toward evading the fight against the enemy • A lack of faith in the political and military leadership or the possibility of victory
3	• Support for the country's participation in the armed conflict • Recognition of the justness of the war, mainly at the ideological level of public consciousness • The presence of individual signs of dissatisfaction with the war • Distrust of the leadership at the socio-psychological (domestic) level
4	• Numerous signs of a "people's war" • Full recognition by the population of the war's justness (the need to participate in an armed conflict) • An expression of unity with the army • Confidence in the leadership of the country and, on the contrary, antagonism toward the enemy

SOURCE: Adapted from Goncharov and Ostroverkhiy, 2021.

---

[51] Goncharov and Ostroverkhiy, 2021.

CHAPTER 2

The Ukraine War and Its Effects on Military Manpower

In this chapter, I describe the effects of the first 18 months of Russia's full-scale invasion of Ukraine. The severe losses of Russian military manpower from the war, which is still in an active phase at the time of this writing, are likely to have lasting effects on the future recruiting and retention of a professional force. In particular, the manner in which Russian commanders have mistreated their personnel suggests the Russian military's reversion to old patterns of wartime command behavior, which are somewhat incompatible with recruiting and retaining professional volunteers. Russia's conduct of its war of choice threatens to undo many of the gains that were made in Russian personnel policies, proficiency, recruiting, and retention in the decade before the war in Ukraine.

Russia's Prewar Expectations and Effects on Military Manpower

On the basis of observable Russian deployments prior to the February 2022 full-scale invasion of Ukraine and Russian soldier accounts, it appears that Kremlin leadership believed its invasion of Ukraine would be lightly contested, at best. As a result of this assumption, military leaders did not prepare or even inform many of the troops about their upcoming operational tasks, which led to severe early losses, operational setbacks, and retreats in the first few months of the war. There is little evidence to suggest that Russia changed its training programs ahead of the invasion to prepare troops for their tasks or to raise proficiency. By not using the time before the war wisely, Russia missed several key opportunities to prepare its forces and the defense industry to produce critical ammunition stockpiles.[1]

Although it is not known precisely when the Kremlin decided to plan for Operation Z, the name of its February 2022 invasion, some inferences are possible based on Russian behaviors in the months before the war. Russian forces deployed vehicles and other equipment to western Russia in spring 2021 for what they called training exercises, but which now are considered to be redeployments to staging areas. This would suggest that a potential Kremlin decision to invade Ukraine (or to at least be prepared to invade Ukraine, if some set of Russian demands was rebuffed) was made possibly as early as spring or summer 2021. During that time, Russian leadership did not take essential steps to ensure that it had recruited enough personnel, or adequately trained and supplied those personnel, for the operation it was about to wage.

There appears to have been no comprehensive effort to increase contract service numbers to fully staff units that would be participating in the war, although there are a few anecdotes of coercive practices within certain units to compel conscripts to convert to contact service.[2] In September 2021, the Russian military announced a new experimental program to call up 38,000 professional reservists from the Southern Military District and 9,000 from the Central Military District, but these numbers were insufficient for the operational tasks at hand or to create a strategic reserve for Russian forces attacking Ukraine.[3] Nor did Russian leadership ensure that all units, partic-

---

[1] Dara Massicot, "What Russia Got Wrong," *Foreign Affairs*, March/April 2023.

[2] Sasha Sivtsova and Kristina Safonova, "'I'm Panicking—Where Is My Child?' Conscript Soldiers Are Being Sent to Fight Against Ukraine, Their Relatives Say. Here's What Their Families Told Meduza," trans. by Sam Breazeale, Meduza, February 25, 2022; Irina Tumakova [Ирина Тумакова], "Mom, I Love You, if There Is a Funeral, Don't Believe It Right Away" ["Мама, я тебя люблю, если будет похоронка, не верь сразу"], UkrRudProm [УкрРудПром], March 4, 2022.

[3] Sam Cranny-Evans, "Understanding Russia's Mobilization," Royal United Services Institute for Defence and Security Studies, September 28, 2022; Ministry of Defense of the Russian Federation [Министерство обороны Российской Федерации], "BARS Reservists Will Gather in 12 Regions of Siberia, the Urals and the Volga Region" ["В 12 регионах Сибири, Урала и Поволжья состоятся Резервисты БАРС соберутся"], January 17, 2022.

ularly those in western and southern Russia, were staffed to adequate levels. In fact, Russian officials noted in the months prior to the war that the military was 9 percent understaffed as of December 2021.[4]

Anecdotes from Russian personnel suggest that some conscripts were coerced into signing contracts in fall 2021. According to relatives of those personnel, one unit issued threats of nightly beatings until a contract was signed, and in another unit, conscripts in the Eastern Military District were forced to carry heavy boxes or sign a contract in fall 2021.[5] According to the Committee of Soldiers' Mothers, other parents sent in formal complaints that their sons were duped into signing a contract or had their status changed against their will and were deployed to Ukraine in February 2022.[6] Sometimes, Russian unit commanders asked for volunteers and peer pressure or the desire for adventure lured some conscripts into signing contracts.[7] Of note, these coercive practices were also observed during Russia's 2014 invasion of Ukraine, when conscripts were also coerced by their commanders to sign contracts to be legally deployable.[8]

The Russian government withheld necessary information from a large percentage of its fighting force, despite being told by multiple senior Western officials that its war plans were known in the months running up to the war.[9] For Kremlin leadership, operational security and masking its inten-

---

[4] Ministry of Defense of the Russian Federation [Министерство обороны Российской Федерации], "An Extended Meeting of the Board of the Ministry of Defense Was Held in Moscow Under the Leadership of the Supreme Commander-in-Chief of the Russian Armed Forces Vladimir Putin" ["В Москве состоялось расширенное заседание коллегии Минобороны под руководством Верховного Главнокомандующего Вооружёнными Силами России Владимира Путина"], December 21, 2021.

[5] Sivtsova and Safonova, 2022; Tumakova, 2022.

[6] Allison Quinn, "Russia Used Beatings and Tricks to Forcibly Send Rookie Troops to Ukraine, Rights Group Says," Daily Beast, February 24, 2022a.

[7] Sasha Sivtsova, "'We Have No Idea Who We're Fighting For': How Russia Threatens Contract Soldiers Who Refuse to Fight in Ukraine," trans. by Sasha Zibrov, Meduza, May 16, 2022.

[8] Laura Mills, "Russian Conscripts Tell of Fears of Being Sent to Ukraine," Associated Press, February 21, 2015.

[9] Michael Schwirtz, Anton Troianovski, Yousur Al-Hlou, Masha Froliak, Adam Entous, and Thomas Gibbons-Neff, "Putin's War," New York Times, December 16, 2022.

tions appeared to outweigh adequate preparation or rehearsals. This mistake was based in part on Russian beliefs that the government of Ukrainian President Volodymyr Zelenskyy would not survive, that the Ukrainian military would not resist, and that the West would not get involved in a significant way.[10]

There are also no indications that meaningful or comprehensive training modifications were made in Russian units to prepare them for their missions or that personnel were even told about the war. For some Special Forces and VDV units, indications that something unusual was happening occurred in November 2021 when, according to a VDV helicopter pilot, commanders "started giving us weapons that weren't normally used in exercises, and armoring the helicopters," yet, the commanders explained nothing.[11] Many units learned of their tasks only a few days in advance.[12] The units that were forward deployed to Belarus and to western Russia reported that they spent one to two months prior to the war in the fields, but as one soldier told his mother, "We weren't going through any training; we stoked the stove and guarded whatever was around: a military vehicle and equipment."[13] This report was from the 74th Guards Separate Motorized Rifle Brigade, one of Russia's more experienced army units that has served in multiple conflicts and was subsequently heavily damaged during failed river crossings in 2022.

There is little evidence to suggest that Russia's forces incorporated relevant operational experience from their 2014 invasion of Ukraine or from operations in Syria for the planning of the 2022 invasion in the first 18 months of war. This is supported, for example, by the failure to create a unified command until months after the invasion or to use ground

---

[10] Massicot, 2023.

[11] Ilya Barabanov [Илья Барабанов], "'If They Put Me on a Combat Helicopter, I Would Have to Kill.' VKS Pilot Escaped from Russia and Spoke to the BBC" ["'Если бы меня посадили на боевой вертолет, мнебы пришлось убивать.' Пилот ВКС сбежал изРоссии и поговорил с Би-би-си"], BBC Russian Service [Русская служба Би-би-си], June 8, 2023.

[12] Mykhaylo Zabrodskyi, Jack Watling, Oleksandr V. Danylyuk, and Nick Reynolds, *Preliminary Lessons in Conventional Warfighting from Russia's Invasion of Ukraine: February–July 2022*, Royal United Services Institute for Defence and Security Studies, November 30, 2022.

[13] Sivtsova, 2022.

teams for battle damage assessment and for assistance with targeting for inbound strikes.[14]

Following a few months of extensive personnel losses in spring 2022, the Russian military also appears to have failed to conduct comprehensive readiness and inventory checks, update reserve rosters, or complete preparatory work for a mobilization to ensure adequate critical supplies based on the chaotic way that the mobilization unfolded in September 2022. This oversight of not using the critical spring and summer months to ready the mobilization base is particularly negligent, given that Russia's mobilization base was largely neglected during the previous decade of reforms.[15]

Instead, Russian officials attempted a more politically palatable volunteer recruiting campaign in summer 2022 to bring volunteers directly into the military. This effort occurred from late spring until formal mobilization was initiated in September 2022. The process ultimately failed to produce enough volunteers, which forced officials to order a partial mobilization in September 2022. Although the intake of 300,000 was largely complete by November 2022, the mobilization remains open-ended as of April 2024.

During and after mobilization began in September 2022, videos and accounts from personnel and their families quickly emerged that suggested systemic problems: multiple instances of personnel with exemptions mobilized and then rejected (or sometimes sent to the front); a lack of supplies; governors asked to supply their regional units directly (which occasionally led to the provision of substandard clothing and protective gear); and an overall lack of vital supplies, such as tourniquets and appropriate boots, or rusty weapons.[16] Only by early 2023 did the mobilization system become more orderly, and Russian officials began to digitize the process to make it more streamlined.

---

[14] Michael Simpson, Adam R. Grissom, Christopher A. Mouton, John P. Godges, and Russell Hanson, *Road to Damascus: The Russian Air Campaign in Syria, 2015 to 2018*, RAND Corporation, RR-A1170-1, 2022.

[15] Samuel Charap, Dara Massicot, Miranda Priebe, Alyssa Demus, Clint Reach, Mark Stalczynski, Eugeniu Han, and Lynn E. Davis, *Russian Grand Strategy: Rhetoric and Reality*, RAND Corporation, RR-4238-A, 2021.

[16] "Russia Sends Mobilized Men to Ukraine Front After Days of Training—Activists," *Moscow Times*, September 27, 2022.

Russian Casualties After 18 Months of War

To understand the pressures the Russian military is facing to recruit sufficient personnel after 18 months of war, it is necessary to briefly describe the scale of the losses that the military has sustained in this time frame. Russian casualty numbers—a combination of those killed and wounded in action—from the war in Ukraine are severe. Although casualty numbers are highly variable depending on the source, a range of estimates is listed for reference. Combat deaths are classified as a state secret in Russia, which criminalizes public discussion of numbers other than those that are provided by the government. Official Russian casualty figures from September 2022, total 5,937, which is artificially low, as proven by open-source research.[17] Then–Chairman of the Joint Chiefs of Staff Mark Milley said in January 2023 that Russia has suffered "significantly well over 100,000" casualties.[18] Publicly available British intelligence figures put the numbers at 175,000–200,000 casualties, of which 40,000–60,000 were killed in action as of February 2023.[19] Ukrainian official estimates of Russian casualties total 189,460 as of late April 2023.[20]

The BBC and Mediazona have attempted to verify the number of Russian personnel killed in action by monitoring Russian social media for funerals or death announcements and the status of cemeteries that are affiliated with the military or mercenary groups. Confirmed deaths, according to BBC and Mediazona methodology, total 31,665 soldiers and PMC personnel as of September 2023, with the caveat that the actual number is higher because

---

[17] Olga Ivshina [Ольга Ившина], "More Than 20,000 Identified Dead: What Is Known About Russian Losses in Ukraine by April" ["Более 20 000 установленных погибших: чтоизвестно о потерях России в Украине к апрелю"], BBC Russian Service [BBC Русская служба], April 14, 2023.

[18] PBS NewsHour, "Defense Secretary Austin and Gen. Milley Hold News Conference in Germany," video, YouTube, January 20, 2023.

[19] Ministry of Defence [@DefenceHQ], "Latest Defence Intelligence update on the situation in Ukraine—17 February 2023. Find out more about the UK government's response: http://ow.ly/JtaU50MUSPj," post on the X platform, February 17, 2023b.

[20] Ministry of Defense of Ukraine, "The Total Combat Losses of the Enemy from 24.02.2022 to 28.04.2023," database, April 28, 2023.

the methods that are used rely on open sources.[21] These numbers account for several months of fighting during Russia's faltering winter 2023 offensive, from which *shock troop tactics* (using waves of poorly trained recruited convicts or mobilized forces in an attempt to overrun Ukrainian positions or to draw fire for artillery strikes) created a high number of casualties. The deaths of mobilized and convict forces increased rapidly during this period as a result of these costly Russian tactics.[22]

To put these figures into the historical context of Russian wars and conflicts, researchers at the Center for Strategic and International Studies noted, "the number of Russian soldiers killed in Ukraine during the first year of the war [February 2022 to February 2023] was likely greater than the entire number of Russian soldiers killed in every war Russia has fought since World War II [WWII] *combined*."[23]

Most losses have occurred within the Ground Forces, VDV, and Special Forces, which disproportionally affected certain groups, such as professional enlisted contract personnel (particularly NCOs) and junior and field-grade officers, in the opening months of the conflict. Since mobilized Russians were drafted into service in November 2022, those personnel and PMC personnel account for most combat deaths from January to May 2023 according to Mediazona methodology.[24] The VDV has experienced more-severe losses than the Ground Forces as a percentage of overall force strength. The VDV's size prewar was six times smaller than the Ground Forces (45,000

---

[21] "Russian Casualties in Ukraine. Mediazona Summary" ["Потери России в войне с Украиной. Сводка Медиазоны"], Mediazona [Медиазона], webpage, updated December 1, 2023.

[22] For example, 60 percent of 1,900 Russian mobilized soldier deaths occurred after January 1, 2023. Russia's 2023 winter offensive was underway by February 2023, after the appointment of Chief of the General Staff Valeriy Gerasimov (Ivshina, 2023).

[23] "These estimates include regular Russian soldiers from the Russian armed forces, Rosgvardiya, Federal Security Service, and Federal Guard Service; fighters from pro-Russian militias, such as the Donetsk People's Militia and Luhansk People's Militia; and contractors from such private military companies as the Wagner Group" (Jones, McCabe, and Palmer, 2023, pp. 5–6).

[24] "Russian Casualties in Ukraine," 2023.

compared with 280,000), yet their loss numbers are similar.[25] Early VDV losses can be explained by mismanagement and the use of the VDV for difficult missions at the start of the war, but loss rates declined sharply after military leadership began conserving VDV forces by fall 2022.[26] The Navy's losses are in the low hundreds, with most losses from the sinking of the *Moskva* cruiser in the Black Sea in 2022. Russian strategic nuclear forces remain unaffected apart from a small number of damaged heavy bombers. The Air Force has lost 25 percent of its SU-25SM3 aircraft in Ukraine (30 of 120 available), along with 20 of 130 Su-34 bombers, and 33 of 120 Ka-52 helicopters; 134 pilots are confirmed killed in action as of April 2023, with the potential for the real number to be higher.[27] Figure 2.1 breaks down the personnel losses.

There are no publicly available official statistics on the number of Russian personnel missing in action. *Novaya Gazeta Europe* searched and found 1,365 soldiers whose relatives are looking for them as of February 2023, with the caveat that the real number could be higher and that these troops could already have been killed in action.[28] More than a year after the start of Russia's full-scale invasion, Russian human rights activists report that there is no improved mechanism to notify families about casualties or missing status, even after mobilization.[29]

---

[25] International Institute for Strategic Studies, *The Military Balance*, Routledge, 2022, Chapter Five: Russia and Eurasia.

[26] Yousur Al-Hlou, Masha Froliak, and Evan Hill, "'Putin Is a Fool': Intercepted Calls Reveal Russian Army in Disarray," *New York Times*, audio trans. by Aleksandra Koroleva and Oksana Nesterenko, September 28, 2022; "Russian Casualties in Ukraine," 2023.

[27] "Russian Casualties in Ukraine. Mediazona Summary," 2023; Justin Bronk, *Russian Combat Air Strengths and Limitations: Lessons from Ukraine*, Center for Naval Analyses, April 2023.

[28] Daria Talanova [Дарья Таланова] and Antonina Asanova [Антонина Асанова], "'My Sister and I Visited All the Morgues'" ["'Мы с сестрой обошли все морги'"], *Novaya Gazeta Europe* [*Новой газеты Европа*], February 27, 2023; "Russia's Vanished Combatants: Thousands of Russian Servicemen Are MIA in Ukraine. Most of Them Are Likely Dead, but Their Families Can Neither Bury Them nor File for State Compensation," Meduza, February 28, 2023.

[29] "Russia's Vanished Combatants," 2023.

FIGURE 2.1

Russian Losses in Ukraine by Service Specialty as of September 2022

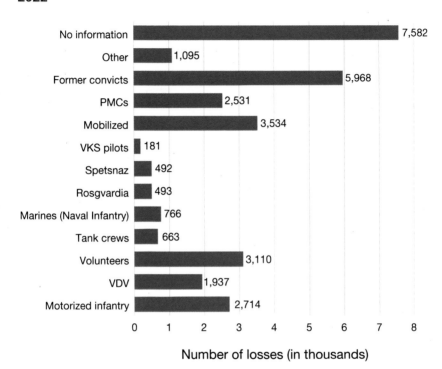

Number of losses (in thousands)

SOURCES: Features information from Ivshina, 2023, and "Russian Casualties in Ukraine. Mediazona Summary," 2023. Personnel losses depicted in Figure 2.1 are as of September 9, 2022.
NOTE: VKS = Aerospace Forces; Rosgvardia = National Guard; Spetznaz = Special Designation Forces.

Effects of Understrength Units on War Planning and Operational Outcomes

Since February 2022, the war in Ukraine has revealed the extent of the manpower shortages within some Russian units. Some of these shortfalls were known before the war—officially, the MOD claimed to be at 91 percent manning as of December 2021, a drop of 4–9 percent since the official numbers of 2017.[30] Russia's manpower issues are now known more precisely thanks to additional information from battlefield performance, recovered military documents obtained by the press and Ukrainian forces, and defector accounts.

Manpower shortages have led to several critical problems for Russia's invasion of Ukraine. The military's first mistake occurred at the outset of the invasion, when its forces were at their strongest in terms of numbers of available troops, equipment, and munitions. The invasion force of an estimated 190,000 personnel was made up of professional enlisted troops from the military, Rosgvardia, PMCs, and fighters called *Kadryovtsy*, who were loyal to Chechen Republic leader Ramzan Kadryov. This invasion force pulled personnel from nearly every Ground Forces and VDV unit, and those forces were sent to Ukraine as battalion tactical groups (BTGs). The International Institute for Strategic Studies estimates that the initial invasion force used around 75 percent of Russia's total deployable land combat forces.[31]

In a departure from Russian doctrine, the invasion force was not organized into a first echelon (attack force) and second echelon (strategic reserve) structure. Instead, all forces were committed mostly at the start of the invasion to multiple axes of attack with no ready strategic reserve. Although the BTG as a formation is designed for certain types of fighting (such as rapid-reaction or rapid-deployment and other low-intensity conflicts), it lacks the necessary organic firepower, logistics, and staffing that larger and heavier formations (such as brigades, regiments, and divisions) have and that were needed for the high-intensity and protracted conflict that Russia

---

[30] In 2017, senior Russian military officials said that the Armed Forces were staffed at 95–100 percent (V. V. Gerasimov [В. В. Герасимов], "On the Progress of Executing the Directives of the President of the Russian Federation from 7 May 2012, Nos. 603, 604 and Development of the Armed Forces of the Russian Federation" ["О ходе выполнения указов Президента Российской Федерации от 7 мая 2012 года N603, 604 и развития Вооруженных Сил Российской Федерации"], *Military Thought* [*Военная мысль*], No. 12, 2017; Ministry of Defense of the Russian Federation, 2021).

[31] At 150,000, the International Institute for Strategic Studies' estimates for the size of the initial invasion force are lower than some other estimates (International Institute for Strategic Studies, 2022, Chapter 5: Russia and Eurasia).

did not plan for but found itself in.[32] The inherent logistical limitations of the BTGs, combined with manpower shortfalls, undermined the technically more modern and capable Russian equipment from the outset.

In the run-up to the invasion, the military's articulated goal was that every Ground Forces regiment or brigade would be able to field two battalions staffed completely with contract personnel and a third with conscripts. According to Chief of the General Staff Gerasimov in 2017, this would enable each division or brigade to have two BTGs available for deployment.[33] Yet, two years later, the Russian media reported that the breakdown of enlisted Ground Forces (the ranks of privates and sergeants) was 53 percent contract service personnel and the remainder conscript, which was not enough for two fully manned BTGs per brigade.[34] This shortfall could be a result of how the MOD recruited during this prewar period. In contrast with the initial contract service recruiting drives of the late 2000s, infantry positions were not prioritized in the MOD's 2013–2020 action plan for contract service recruiting; instead, the MOD focused on specialist positions during those years.[35] As Jonas Kjellén of the Swedish Defence Research Agency pointed out, this emphasis might have left essential infantry positions unfilled within Ground Forces units by 2022.[36]

Other positions that were filled by conscripts in peacetime could not be filled the same way in wartime, which worsened the manpower shortages for Russian forces when they were operationally deployed. A major selling point of professional contract service recruitment, as voiced by military leaders, was that experienced professionals were needed to operate advanced

---

[32] Lester W. Grau and Charles K. Bartles, "Getting to Know the Russian Battalion Tactical Group," Royal United Services Institute for Defence and Security Studies, April 14, 2022.

[33] Gerasimov, 2017.

[34] "Gives Us a Winning Point" ["дает нам победное очко"], Weapons of Russia [Оружие России], October 19, 2019.

[35] No updated action plan has been publicly available after 2020 (Ministry of Defense of the Russian Federation, undated-a).

[36] Jonas Kjellén, *Bringing the Soldier Back In: Russian Military Manning, Manpower, and Mobilisation in the Light of Russia's War in Ukraine*, Swedish Defence Research Agency, March 2023.

technical equipment, such as communications or electronic warfare equipment, and unskilled positions (in the Russian military, this means cooks and drivers) were to be filled by defense contractors or conscripts.[37] Per Kremlin policy, a conscript cannot serve in a war zone unless they have had at least four months of basic training, and this restriction has de facto been extended to no conscript can serve in combat at all. These support services are, of course, essential during a combat deployment, which suggests that other contract service personnel are filling these positions in Ukraine at the expense of other positions and worsening the manpower problem.

Recovered Russian military personnel rosters in occupied Ukraine reveal that unit manpower strength was too low, which likely negatively affected Russian military performance. For example, in April 2022, the UAF recovered the complete roster of one brigade that was considered to be at high readiness: the 136th Separate Guards Motorized Rifle Brigade from the Southern Military District. The roster paints a picture of a unit that was staffed fairly well between conscript and contract service: 83 percent contract service and 17 percent conscript billets. The brigade maintained two motorized rifle battalions that were fully staffed with contract service personnel and one multiple rocket launcher battalion, as per requirements. The third motorized rifle brigade was 60 percent conscript, as would be expected. The signal, maintenance, tank, and reconnaissance units were majority contract as well.[38] However, a closer read reveals problems. Overall, the brigade was understaffed at only 85 percent of total authorized strength, which meant that 15 percent of authorized billets were empty, and

---

[37] Charles K. Bartles, "Russian Armed Forces: Enlisted Professionals," *NCO Journal*, March 2019.

[38] Analysis of the 136th Separate Motorized Rifle Brigade can be found at Henry Schlottman [@HN_Schlottman], "Last month, ▬ military intel posted what appeared to be a complete roster of ▬ 136th Separate Guards Motorized Rifle Brigade. It helpfully provided info for contract vs conscript personnel (rare) which I've broken down by subunit in this graphic," post on the X platform, April 23, 2022, who cites information recovered by the Main Intelligence Directorate [Головне Управління Розвідки], "War Criminals—Servicemen of the 136th Separate Motorized Rifle Brigade Committing War Crimes Against the Civilian Population of Ukraine" ["Военные преступники—военнослужащие 136 отдельной мотострелковой бригады совершающие военные преступления против мирного населения Украины"], Ministry of Defense Ukraine [Міністерства Оборони України], March 18, 2022.

the conscripts could not be deployed to Ukraine according to presidential guidance. Furthermore, the engineering battalion, which is vital for a rapid assault into enemy territory, was only 66 percent contract, which meant that 34 percent of its personnel could not be sent into Ukraine.

Understrength units and partially crewed vehicles at the war's outset undermined combat performance and survivability in combat. For example, basic steps, such as dismounted infantry to protect armored columns and proper reconnaissance to clear and prepare routes in advance, were not conducted and possibly contributed to multiple ambushes in rural and urban terrain.[39] The reasons for these oversights are not known, although their occurrence suggests a war plan that prioritized the speed of advance over proper route clearance or that the military lacked available personnel to fully crew the equipment. The result of these oversights included multiple Russian units caught in ambushes and traps, which led to destroyed columns, heavy losses, and blocked routes, particularly in the north, derailing what Russian leadership had designed to be a lightning advance into northern, eastern, and southern Ukraine. This decision to prioritize speed over route clearance disregarded important lessons from Russia's own military history. During the invasion of Afghanistan, the Soviet Union installed a network of permanent checkpoints at regular intervals for route clearance and maintenance within two months of its invasion, which absorbed an estimated 20–25 percent of overall deployed manpower to sustain.[40]

By summer 2022, Russian deployed forces had sustained severe attrition. Although measuring the exact number of casualties and equipment losses is difficult because of a lack of high-fidelity data, evidence suggests that some units had to be completely withdrawn to Russia or far behind the front lines in occupied Ukraine until they could be reconstituted. However, most Russian units have been kept in place for 18 months, even when their attrition levels would have classified them as only partially mission

---

[39] Sam Cranny-Evans and Sidharth Kaushal, "Not Out of the Woods Yet: Assessing the Operational Situation in Ukraine," Royal United Services Institute for Defence and Security Studies, March 14, 2022; Rob Lee [@RALee85], "Photos from a destroyed Russian convoy in Chernihiv . . . ," post on the X platform, March 9, 2022.

[40] Rodric Braithwaite, *Afgantsy: The Russians in Afghanistan 1979–89*, Oxford University Press, 2011, p. 140.

capable. Russian military science defines combat capacity according to the following thresholds:

- fully combat-ready units maintain at least 75 percent of their organizational structure
- limited combat-ready units have 50–75 percent of their structure
- partially combat-ready units have 30–50 percent of their structure
- non-combat–ready units have less than 30 percent of their structure.[41]

For example, according to abandoned military documents that were recovered by Ukrainian forces and Western media in 2022 and reviewed by RAND researchers, the chaotic retreat of Russian forces from the Kharkiv region in early fall 2022 shows a variation in available unit manpower or manning levels.[42] Prior to the retreat, the 11th Army Corps was stationed near Balakliia in northeastern Ukraine.[43] This grouping had 71 percent of its authorized manpower on hand at the time of the Ukrainian counter-offensive into Kharkiv, which rendered it limited combat-ready or close to fully combat-ready.[44] Most of the long-range artillery subunits were at 90–100 percent manning. However, key combat subunits, such as motorized rifle battalions, were at 60 percent, and its engineering unit was at 56 percent.[45] Another unit in Kharkiv, the 200th Motorized Rifle Brigade, lost 70 percent of its equipment, 40 percent of its prewar personnel, and a majority of its officers, rendering it non–mission capable (per Russian classifications but not wartime practice) according to recovered documents

---

[41] Ministry of Defense of the Russian Federation [Министерство обороны Российской Федерации], "Combat Readiness" ["Боеспособность"], undated-b.

[42] Mari Saito, Maria Tsvetkova, and Anton Zverev, "Abandoned Russian Base Holds Secrets of Retreat in Ukraine," Reuters, October 26, 2022.

[43] Saito, Tsvetkova, and Zverev, 2022.

[44] Encyclopedia of the Strategic Missile Forces [Энциклопедия РВСН], "Combat Capacity" [БОЕВАЯ СПОСОБНОСТЬ], webpage, 2013.

[45] Saito, Tsvetkova, and Zverev, 2022; 11th Army Corps, "Combat and Personnel Composition of the Balakiliia Force Grouping as of August 2022," trans. by Clinton Reach and Yuliya Shokh, September 2022.

and media interviews with Ukrainian commanders who engaged that brigade in combat.[46]

Personnel Misuse and Maltreatment

In this section, I outline observed problems or factors from February 2022 to September 2023 that are likely to undermine future recruiting and retention. The war in Ukraine has revealed that several pervasive problems in Russian command style and unit discipline remain unresolved despite more than a decade of reform attempts. These problems, while managed or hidden during peacetime, became pronounced in wartime conditions. These issues include a breakdown in order and discipline, inadequate preparation and provisioning of troops, and the perception of indifferent or abusive commanders that has resulted in faltering unit cohesion. These behaviors broke trust relationships and beliefs held by some professional soldiers that the military was competent or was becoming more professional.[47] Prior to the war, the Russian military studied and surveyed its soldiers about factors that contribute to mental resilience and morale in combat conditions. Two Russian strategists noted in 2015 that the following factors were particularly important:

- personal belief in the conflict
- faith in commanders
- hatred of the enemy and confidence in superiority over the enemy
- general well-being
- understanding upcoming actions in battle.[48]

---

[46] Greg Miller, Mary Ilyushina, Catherine Belton, Isabelle Khurshudyan, and Paul Sonne, "'Wiped Out': War in Ukraine Has Decimated a Once Feared Russian Brigade," *Washington Post*, December 16, 2022.

[47] Al-Hlou, Froliak, and Hill, 2022.

[48] S. V. Goncharov [С. В. Гончаров] and O. G. Zaets [О. Г. Заец], "Assessment and Accounting of the Moral and Psychological Factor When Commanders Make Decisions Using Automated Troop Control Systems" ["Оценка и учет морально-психологического фактора при принятии командирами решений с

Many of those factors are being undermined by how Russia is commanding its forces in Ukraine, and this maltreatment could have lasting consequences on the willingness of Russia's professional enlisted personnel to remain in service.

Russian soldiers have experienced basic problems, such as wage arrears, absent or hostile commanders, and, at times, a lack of adequate food and water. Wage arrears have frequently popped up for *contractniki* and mobilized personnel throughout the war according to multiple accounts, but it is difficult to ascertain the pervasiveness of this problem.[49] At times, base salaries are paid but not combat pay bonuses or sign-on bonuses.[50] In a few cases, soldiers have found that they were not paid at all, and the processes to appeal for compensation are cumbersome.

From the very start of the war, there were signs that order, discipline, and trust were broken, as large parts of the invasion force were lied to about whether they would be sent to Ukraine.[51] In the run-up to the invasion, many professional contract service personnel from across Russia were told that they were being sent forward for training exercises and informed about combat deployment only three days in advance according to soldier accounts.[52] Others thought that the deployments to the Ukrainian border were attempts at coercing concessions from the West, not for an actual war. Belarusians who watched the buildup noticed that Russian soldiers were

---

использованием автоматизированных систем управления войсками"], *Military Thought* [*Военная мысль*], No. 8, 2015.

[49] Anton Gerashchenko, "Part 195. 'I Thought They Would Pay, but Damn'" ["Часть 195. 'Думал будут платить, а нихера'"], video, YouTube, April 13, 2022; Allison Quinn, "'There Is Such F---ery Going on Here': Russian Soldiers 'Revolting' as They Get Stiffed on Ukraine Payouts," Daily Beast, April 13, 2022b.

[50] Robert Coalson, "'I Didn't Think I'd Survive': Russian Volunteer Soldier Who Quit Ukraine War Recalls His Ordeal," Radio Free Europe/Radio Liberty, November 9, 2022.

[51] "'My Soul Is in My Own Hands': The Case of the First Russian Officer Charged with a Felony for Refusing to Kill in Ukraine," trans. by Anna Razumnaya, Meduza, December 27, 2022.

[52] Sivtsova, 2022.

drinking a lot and selling their diesel fuel, which suggested that the troops did not think they would need those supplies for combat operations.[53]

This deception did not stop at enlisted personnel and junior officers. According to field work conducted by the Royal United Services Institute, even battalion commanders and some flag officers in the general staff were kept in the dark about the invasion plans until just days in advance.[54] As a result, much of the force had limited time to interpret complicated orders and did not have time to coordinate with other units.[55] Recovered documents obtained by the *New York Times* from the 76th Guards Air Assault Division (a unit at the forefront of the attack on Kyiv that is also accused of war crimes in Bucha) reveals intricately planned timetables for various units to reach their destinations, as if there was no possibility for resistance along those routes.[56]

According to defector accounts, personnel who did have advance knowledge of the operation were told that the war would be over in days and would not be significantly contested by the UAF. Their commanders led them to believe that they could seize Kyiv "in seven days, without firing a shot," according to an intercepted call from one soldier to his mother released by the Ukrainian government.[57] Instead, that soldier's unit took fire outside the Chernobyl zone and discovered that the Ukrainians had taken down all the road signs to Kyiv in anticipation of the offensive, but the unit had not been provided with maps. Another soldier noted a similar experience when he was deployed to the Ukrainian border in February 2022. He was told that the deployment was for training but when he arrived, he realized it was in

---

[53] "'They Drink a Lot, Sell Their Fuel': Belarusians Give Low Marks to Russian Troops Deployed for Drills," Radio Free Europe/Radio Liberty, February 19, 2022. Prewar in Belarus: "'The soldiers have settled in the surrounding forests,' the local, who asked not to be identified, added. 'They drink a lot and sell a lot of their diesel fuel. They are living in tents.'"

[54] Zabrodskyi et al., 2022.

[55] "'My Soul Is in My Own Hands,'" 2022; Schwirtz et al., 2022; Zabrodskyi et al., 2022.

[56] Schwirtz et al., 2022.

[57] Erika Kinetz, "'Never Saw Such Hell': Russian Soldiers in Ukraine Call Home," Associated Press, February 24, 2023.

preparation for war: "I think lots of us imagined that it would be just like Crimea—that everything would happen peacefully."[58]

These assumptions fell apart after the war began and Russian troops found that the UAF had made preparations and were fighting back. According to Russian soldiers' accounts from intercepted phone calls over the first seven months of the war released by the Ukrainian government, the troops directed their anger at their command, claiming they had been deceived. For many units encountering this shock, the damage to their trust and belief in the Russian military's competence was immediate. The intercepted phone calls revealed how many Russian commanders "warned us [the troops] one day before we left" and how the troops felt "fooled like little kids" from being deceived: "They said we were going to training. These bastards didn't tell us anything."[59] Other units noted inadequate supplies: "They [the command] didn't tell us it was going to be like this. They told us we were going to do some training exercises. We didn't have sufficient equipment. There were no helmets or armor. There was no food or water."[60]

This pattern of deceiving soldiers about upcoming combat deployments and missions also occurred in previous Soviet and Russian operations. According to personnel accounts, some Soviet soldiers were not told that they were deploying to Afghanistan in 1979 until they disembarked from an aircraft and discovered they had arrived at a staging base near the border with Afghanistan.[61] During Russia's 2014 invasion of Ukraine, limited soldier accounts suggest that those soldiers and their families were also not aware they would be deployed to Ukraine until a few days in advance.[62]

Faltering unit cohesion coincided with logistical failures and a lack of food, water, and shelter. Russian troops—particularly the contract service personnel—have faced supply problems in the first year of the war, under-

---

[58] "'My Soul Is in My Own Hands,'" 2022.

[59] Al-Hlou, Froliak, and Hill, 2022.

[60] "'They Told Us Nobody's Going to Take Us Home': Russian Soldiers Held Captive in Luhansk Region for Refusing to Fight in Ukraine," Meduza, July 22, 2022.

[61] Svetlana Alexievich, *Boys in Zinc*, Penguin Books, 2017.

[62] Glenn Kates, "In Russia, Ukraine Conflict Hits Home with Secret Funerals, Missing Men," Radio Free Europe/Radio Liberty, August 28, 2014; Steven Rosenberg, "Ukraine Crisis: Forgotten Death of Russian Soldier," BBC News, September 18, 2014.

mining soldiers' morale, will to fight, and faith in their commanders. In the early weeks of the war, when Russian forces were on the offensive, the logistics convoys were often attacked and could not keep the troops supplied. Some troops simply found the rations unsatisfactory and their commanders permitted them to loot.[63] Two weeks into the invasion, Russian soldiers were seen stealing chickens to eat.[64] In other cases, troops were provided food that had expired seven years prior.[65] Inadequate clothing led to frostbite.[66] These supply issues are reminiscent of problems that were seen in previous Russian conflicts in Afghanistan and Chechnya. In Afghanistan, Soviet troops had poor shelter, had infrequent opportunities to bathe or launder clothing, and lacked nutritious food to the point of scurvy, with some personnel (including nurses) losing teeth from malnutrition.[67] Mobilization in September 2022 remedied many of these issues by summer 2023.

Russian soldiers have expressed frustration or at times disgust with their leadership in occupied Ukraine. Officers stealing the contents of care packages was such a common occurrence for one unit in summer 2022 that soldiers told their families not to bother sending anything.[68] Other officers disappeared for days in the early months of the war, and after the High Mobility Artillery Rocket System was introduced to Ukraine, senior

---

[63] "'We continue to see indications that the Russians did not properly plan for logistics and sustainment,' [Pentagon Press Secretary John F.] Kirby said. 'We know that they continue to have fuel issues across their force, and that they're still struggling with food.' He noted that there is footage of Russian troops ransacking grocery stores in Ukraine. The Russians 'either didn't properly plan for logistics and sustainment or they didn't properly execute to their plan, but they are still having problems,' he said" (Jim Garamone, "Russian Forces Invading Ukraine Suffer Low Morale," U.S. Department of Defense, March 23, 2022).

[64] NSU [НГУ] [@ng_ukraine], "Hungry Russian soldiers steal chickens from a private household in #Ukraine," post on the X platform, March 9, 2022.

[65] V. Cheianov, Esq. [@cheianov], "Captured Russian army field rations," post on the X platform, February 28, 2022.

[66] Al-Hlou, Froliak, and Hill, 2022.

[67] Alexievich, 2017; Braithwaite, 2011, p. 122.

[68] Gerashchenko, 2022.

officers relocated their command posts well away from the frontlines.[69] By fall 2022, volunteers and mobilized personnel began to complain about old equipment being sent to the front, such as rifles with crooked muzzles or weapons that would jam easily.[70] Soldiers expressed frustration in September 2022 that "everything here is ancient, not modern like on Zvezda [a state-run Russian military channel]."[71]

Other contract service personnel have expressed their belief that their commanders do not care about them at all and are indifferent to casualties. This is a problem that is destructive to trust and retention, and a problem that seems to have been pervasive from the start of the operation. One paratrooper from the 331st Guards Airborne Regiment noted in September 2022 that "there were 400 paratroopers. And only 38 of them survive. . . . Because our commanders sent soldiers to the slaughter."[72] Another contract serviceman, who wants to resign but has been unable because of Russian laws extending contracts until the SMO has concluded, said this about service conditions in early 2023:

> They treat you like cattle. . . . There are very few decent commanders; everybody's afraid, nobody wants to die. There's not enough grub. Casualties every day. On the news, everything is so rosy. But in reality, there are problems with communications, problems with supplies. It's not like it seems.[73]

---

[69] CIT (en) [@CITeam_en], "This rare video was filmed by a (non-captured) Russian soldier complaining about losses and harsh conditions," post on the X platform, March 3, 2022; "Russians Have Adapted to HIMARS. What Are Ukraine's Alternatives?" *Euromaidan Press*, January 9, 2023.

[70] Coalson, 2022.

[71] Al-Hlou, Froliak, and Hill, 2022.

[72] Al-Hlou, Froliak, and Hill, 2022.

[73] Novaya Vkladka, "'They Drink Out of Fear': A Dispatch from the Closed Russian Military Village Where Six Draftees Have Died Since Mobilization Began," trans. by Sam Breazeale, Meduza, February 22, 2023.

Refusals and Resignations

Russian servicemen have tried to resign or leave military service since the start of the invasion of Ukraine. Although it is difficult to capture the pervasiveness of this issue, Russian officials' efforts to manage the problem through legislation and increased penalties suggest that it is concerning to authorities. In the opening months of the invasion, legal loopholes had not yet been closed, and officers and contract service personnel could still legally resign on moral grounds without criminal prosecution.[74] According to the independent Russian media outlet Meduza, the most common reasons cited for terminating contracts during the first seven months of the war were "philosophical opposition to the war," status as the sole breadwinner in the family, and "systematic violation of the terms of the contract by the military command."[75] The resignation process involved submitting a letter to a commanding officer, who would then have to begin a lengthy discharge process that involved the commander writing to officials as high up as the military district command.[76]

Sometimes the contract termination requests were granted, but other times, the commanding officers took the letters but did not process the requests. If the resignations were accepted, the soldiers had to find their own way back to Russia, according to soldier accounts.[77] The soldiers whose

---

[74] According to human rights activist Sergei Krivenko, "If a soldier acts according to such procedures, then he cannot be criminally prosecuted for this. Because there are no criminal articles for requesting the termination of a contract based on anti-war beliefs. The soldier is in the unit, he's not running away anywhere. And that means he can't be prosecuted for desertion or going AWOL [absent without leave]" (Timofei Rozhanskiy, "Why Russian Soldiers Are Refusing to Fight in the War in Ukraine," Radio Free Europe/Radio Liberty, July 20, 2022).

[75] "'I Go to War in My Sleep': Russia Is Failing to Provide PTSD Support for Soldiers Returning from Ukraine. Psychiatrists Expect Disaster," trans. by Sam Breazeale, Meduza, January 26, 2023; "'They Told Us Nobody's Going to Take Us Home,'" 2022.

[76] According to Article 51, paragraph six of the federal Law on Military Duty and Military Service, there must be a "good reason" for dismissal. As human rights activists note, a "good reason" is understood legally "as circumstances that objectively prevent the contract soldier from fully fulfilling the terms of the contract" (Sivtsova, 2022).

[77] Anna Pavlova, "When Soldiers Say No. Hundreds of Russian Servicemen Face Trial in Defiance of Ukraine Deployment, Mediazona Study Reveals," Mediazona, April 11, 2023.

requests were accepted reported that when they resigned, their commanders used various methods to dissuade them, such as threatening court martials and prison time or stalling their transport back to Russia.[78] Some personnel who resigned, when it was still possible before the September 2022 mobilization, had their identification documents stamped with such language as "prone to treachery, deceit, and lies," or they were discharged for failing to fulfill the terms of their contract.[79] These actions could make it difficult to get federal employment, but the actions could be appealed.[80] Soldiers reported to their families in the summer of 2022 that resignations were no longer being accepted, months before the law officially was changed.[81]

Military units in Russia tried to embarrass personnel who resigned or refused orders in 2022 by creating "walls of shame" with their pictures.[82] Other soldiers were sent to holding facilities in occupied Ukraine (some in windowless basements) or to a camp for objectors, where they were intimidated or beaten by guards.[83] In one account, a soldier who had resigned on moral grounds told his father that he was taken to a holding facility and informed that he could either return to his unit or transfer to a different unit, but he had to remain.[84]

Resignations can also become infectious. Several recovered resignation letters suggest that professional enlisted personnel sometimes resigned

---

[78] Pavlova, 2023; Rozhanskiy, 2022.

[79] Katerina Orlova, "'Freeing Them from the Motherland's Tenacious Grip. Russian Soldiers Are Refusing to Fight in Ukraine. Lawyer Maxim Grebenyuk Is Helping Defend Their Rights," trans. by Sian Glaessner, Meduza, May 3, 2022b.

[80] Vladimir Sevrinovsky, "'Refusing to Kill People Isn't a Crime': The Russian National Guard Is Firing Officers Who Refuse to Join the War in Ukraine," trans. by Sam Breazeale, Meduza, March 29, 2022.

[81] "'I Go to War in My Sleep,'" 2023; "'They Told Us Nobody's Going to Take Us Home,'" 2022.

[82] Rozhanskiy, 2022.

[83] "'I Go to War in My Sleep,'" 2023; "'They Told Us Nobody's Going to Take Us Home,'" 2022.

[84] "'They Told Us Nobody's Going to Take Us Home,'" 2022; "'I Go to War in My Sleep,'" 2023.

on the same day and used identical language.[85] According to one soldier's mother, 11 refusals allegedly grew to 250 in the 74th Guards Separate Motorized Rifle Brigade in March 2022. The unit was reportedly threatened by FSB officers and military prosecutors until they retracted their resignations. This unit would go on to take severe losses—one battalion—in the failed crossing of the Siverskyi Donets River in May 2022.[86]

The Russian government closed many of the loopholes to resignation by fall 2022, when it declared mobilization, and criminal consequences were imposed for refusing or disobeying orders. Around 30 cases were brought against personnel from September 2022 to April 2023 (a small percentage of overall manpower) with an average sentence of 20 months to four years of prison time for "disobeying orders," according to Mediazona analysis of Russian court documents.[87] For "collective disobedience" the sentence was longer on average: three to four years. As Mediazona's research suggests, refusals carry the lightest sentence compared with going AWOL, deserting, or assaulting an officer, which suggests that objectors in the military might want to take this path.[88] Other penalties in the Russian criminal code have been increased, such as six years for looting and ten years for voluntarily surrendering to the Ukrainians.[89]

Desertions and Going AWOL

Desertion, going AWOL, failure to obey orders, and violence against superiors is a growing problem 18 months post-invasion but still at small numbers

---

[85] Mark Krutov [@kromark], "Soldiers from the 1st Motor Rifle Regiment, part of elite Russian unit, 2nd Guards Tamanskaya Motor Rifle Division (Kalininets, Moscow region) . . . ," post on the X platform, September 12, 2022; Bogdan Voron [@Bogdan_Voron], "The Ukrainian army servicemen found a pile of 'refusers' reports . . . ," post on the X platform, September 19, 2022.

[86] Anton Troianovski and Marc Santora, "Growing Evidence of a Military Disaster on the Donets Pierces a Pro-Russian Bubble," *New York Times*, May 15, 2022.

[87] Pavlova, 2023.

[88] Pavlova, 2023.

[89] Ivan Nechepurenko and John Ismay, "Russian Lawmakers Toughen Penalties for Soldiers as Moscow Appears to Signal a Possible Escalation," *New York Times*, September 20, 2022; Pavlova, 2023; "Russia Toughens Penalty for Voluntary Surrender, Refusal to Fight," Radio Free Europe/Radio Liberty, September 24, 2022.

overall. It is hard to quantify the full extent of the problem, but it is possible to quantify the cases that make it to the final stages of the Russian judicial process. Desertion, defined in Russian law as the intent to permanently leave one's military unit to avoid military duty, carries a stiffer penalty than going AWOL for less than 30 days. Collective acts of desertion carry a stiffer penalty (5 to 15 years) than individual desertion. Assaulting a commander can lead to convictions of five to six years. Eight mobilized soldiers who deserted their unit together in Luhansk after they received no food and their commanding officer threatened to "shoot and bury any soldiers who dishonored the unit" now face 5- to 15-year prison sentences.[90]

Going AWOL carries less punishment than desertion, sometimes a year or less depending on the circumstances. Reliable information on the scale of this problem across the Russian frontlines is not available. Some units reportedly catch deserters and return them quickly without reporting their absence or detain deserters in temporary and often crude locations (such as a pit in the ground or in a cellar).[91] It is possible that some of this information is not reported up the chain of command for fear of reprisal, and, if the information is reported, it would almost certainly be sensitive or classified and not made public. At the other end of the spectrum of deserters, there is a percentage that are prosecuted in the Russian court system, although it is impossible to say how many. From January to July 2023, 2,076 AWOL cases were recorded, mostly among mobilized personnel; this number is less than 1 percent of the total mobilized soldiers.[92] Of the cases that received sentencing, around half of the sentences were suspended so that the soldiers could be immediately sent back to the front.[93] According to Mediazona, reports on sentencing for desertion, going AWOL, or other violations are disseminated to most unit commanders as a military-wide report. As

---

[90] Pavlova, 2023.

[91] Carl Schreck, "'Simply Medieval': Russian Soldiers Held in Pits and Cellars for Refusing to Fight in Ukraine," Radio Free Europe/Radio Liberty, July 15, 2023.

[92] "One Hundred Convictions a Week. Over Two Thousand AWOL Cases Went to Courts in the First Half of 2023, Primarily Against Mobilised Soldiers" ["Сто приговоров в неделю. За полгода в суды поступило больше двух тысяч дел о самоволке—в основном против мобилизованных"], Mediazona [Медиазона], July 19, 2023.

[93] Pavlova, 2023.

a method of intimidation, arrests of those who refuse to serve are made in front of the unit and, increasingly, the units (often made up of conscripts) are forced to watch the trial.[94]

Political Officers Fail to Increase Patriotism or Halt War Crimes

As noted in Chapter 1, Russia's Political–Military Directorate was reestablished in 2019 within the MOD. One of the directorate's missions is to educate military personnel about their obligations under the Geneva Convention and other laws of war. Its primary mission is to increase patriotism, loyalty, and compliance with the Kremlin's orders and worldview. Political officers are present at each echelon from company level and above, within Russian units in occupied Ukraine, based on an analysis of personnel files obtained by Ukrainian intelligence.[95] Based on the United Nations' March 2023 findings that Russian forces committed widespread war crimes during this period, it would appear that political officers' instruction on the laws of war were wholly inadequate.[96]

Prior to the 2022 invasion, it appears that political officers had some effect on convincing the rank and file that they would be greeted as liberators in Ukraine and that the troops would be "liberating" Ukraine from a "nazi" government. Intercepted phone calls from the first few months after the invasion, released by the Ukrainian government, suggest that some Russian soldiers believed they would encounter fascists and nazis in Ukraine but instead encountered a military defending its country.[97] Ukrainian civil-

---

[94] Pavlova, 2023.

[95] For example, two recovered personnel logs from separate units, the 11th Army Corps and the 20th Motorized Rifle Division, had political officers (often in deputy commander positions) at division or brigade headquarter levels, all the way down to the company level. Of the 20th Motorized Rifle Division's 469 officer billets, 31 billets were political officers according to the unit roster (Main Intelligence Directorate [Головне Управління Розвідки], "List of Personnel of the 20th Guards Motorized Rifle Division of the Armed Forces of the Russian Federation" ["Список особового складу 20-ї гвардійської мотострілецької дивізії ЗС РФ], Ministry of Defense Ukraine [Міністерства Оборони України], March 2, 2022).

[96] United Nations Human Rights Council, *Report of the Independent International Commission of Inquiry on Ukraine*, A/HRC/52/62, advance unedited version, March 15, 2023.

[97] Orlova, 2022b.

ians describe Russian soldiers going door to door looking for nazis and *banderites*, a term used pejoratively to mean fascists (and linked to members and supporters of the radical wing of the WWII-era Organization of Ukrainian Nationalists).[98] When the reality they faced was different, the soldiers told their families about the deception: "We haven't seen a single fascist here. . . . This war is based on a false pretense. No one needed it. We got here and people were living normal lives. Very well, like in Russia. And now they have to live in basements."[99]

There has been persistent confusion and disillusionment among some Russian contract soldiers about why they were deployed to Ukraine, at least in the opening months of the war. One soldier noted in an intercepted phone call that the invasion was one of the "stupidest decisions our government has ever made."[100] Another said, "we have no idea who we're fighting against or fighting for, or how we're doing it."[101] Efforts to increase patriotism and loyalty within the units fighting in Ukraine since the invasion is mixed, and there are few signs that political officers can improve unit cohesion, morale, or proficiency, given the rate of casualties, the insertion of mobilized forces, and the detached unit leadership. As one human rights lawyer for contract servicemen put it, a soldier might have gone into Ukraine thinking they would "de-Nazify" and "demilitarize," but

> when a soldier understands that the reality is that you can be killed, at any moment, for many this is a sobering thought. Many start to reconsider their need to participate. Because Ukrainians know what they are dying for, that's what their fearlessness is rooted in. When our grandfathers fought [in WWII], they knew what they were dying for. But not all of our soldiers understand why their deaths are necessary.[102]

---

[98] Isabelle Khurshudyan and Michael Robinson Chavez, "Ukrainian Villagers Describe Cruel and Brutal Russian Occupation," *Washington Post*, April 4, 2022; Erika Kinetz, Oleksandr Stashevskyi, and Vasilisa Stepanenko, "How Russian Soldiers Ran a 'Cleansing' Operation in Bucha, Ukraine," PBS, November 3, 2022.

[99] Al-Hlou, Froliak, and Hill, 2022.

[100] Al-Hlou, Froliak, and Hill, 2022.

[101] Sivtsova, 2022.

[102] Orlova, 2022b.

By October 2022, political officers began to distribute a new booklet called "Memo to Russian Armed Forces Serviceman Participating in the Special Military Operation" to personnel. This booklet framed the conflict as a fight against a corrupt, degenerate West that wants to plunge Russia into "chaos and anarchy, destroy its statehood, and dismember it. . . . [T]heir goal is to turn us into a resource that they can use to support their dying civilization."[103] It also falsely claimed that the Zelenskyy government is a "Nazi regime" and that Ukraine "never had a strong tradition of true state-hood." The booklet includes multiple paraphrased lines from Stalin's WWII-era Order No. 227 outlawing retreats, with recognizable slogans such as "Not One Step Back!"[104] Contract service personnel who were interviewed said that they do not think highly of these materials and do not read them. One of them said:

> I've had things like [this booklet] in my pocket for seven years, just because I had to. I've only ever opened it to update the command staff printed on the first page: when it changes, we're supposed to glue a new page into the booklet, or at least mark the changes with a pencil. They watch us, to make sure we do it.[105]

Structurally, the way many units are organized has created a situation in which no single unit commander feels that they are accountable for war crimes or other atrocities committed by their subordinates. This is because ensuring compliance with the laws of war and training the troops about that conduct are the political officer's job, but the political officer has no authority, let alone respect, among the troops.[106] Therefore, the task of ensuring compliance with international law might have fallen through the cracks with disastrous results for the Ukrainian military and civilians who are captured by Russian personnel. The United Nations has found evidence of

---

[103] Lilia Yapparova, "'Not a Single Step Back!' In a Booklet Issued to Soldiers, the Russian Authorities Denounce the Army's 'Shameful' Retreat from Kherson and Urge a Return to 'Stalinist Methods,'" trans. by Sam Breazeale, Meduza, April 5, 2023.

[104] Yapparova, 2023.

[105] Yapparova, 2023.

[106] Main Intelligence Directorate, 2022.

systemic war crimes and atrocities committed by Russian military personnel and Russian proxy forces in occupied Ukraine since 2022. A report from the United Nations Human Rights Council noted that

> Russian authorities have committed a wide range of violations of international human rights law and international humanitarian law in many regions of Ukraine and in the Russian Federation. Many of these amount to war crimes and include [willful] killings, attacks on civilians, unlawful confinement, torture, rape, and forced transfers and deportations of children,

as well as "indiscriminate attacks" harming civilians.[107]

---

[107] United Nations Human Rights Council, 2023, p. 1.

CHAPTER 3

Wartime Modifications to Recruiting and Retention Policy

This chapter presents a description of Russian official's attempts to recruit and retain military personnel during the first 18 months of its full-scale invasion of Ukraine. The potential long-term effects on recruiting and retention when the active phase of the war concludes were considered. The success of these manpower efforts will be highly contingent on the future Russian economy, public support for the military as an institution, and the outcome of a war that is still in progress at the time of writing.

Attempts to Recover from Personnel Losses in Ukraine

Expanding Eligibility for Recruits by Modifying Admission Standards

Prior to the war, eligible men between the ages of 18 and 40 who passed physical and mental health checks and who had no serious criminal records (such as violent crimes or felonies) were eligible for professional military service.[1] Not all men were healthy enough to serve; prior to the 2022 invasion, between 22 percent and 27 percent of those who were called up for

---

[1] Moscow Mayor's Office [Официальный сайт Мэра Москвы], "How to Enroll in Military Service Under a Contract" ["Военная служба по контракту"], webpage, undated.

conscription were deemed unfit for service.[2] The Russian military appears to have lowered many admission standards as its manpower needs became acute in 2022—a practice that is not uncommon for militaries during wartime. To expand the pool of volunteers, the Russian military raised the maximum age limit (from 40 to 65) for those who wished to volunteer in 2022.[3] The requirement for a clean criminal record was dropped; now, only child molestation, treason, espionage, and terrorism are disqualifying crimes.[4] Violent felonies, such as rape and murder, no longer disqualify someone from military service according to the 2022 modifications.[5] During the chaotic mobilization of September 2022, some men with disabilities or poor health were mobilized, which suggests that physical standards were also lowered.[6]

By summer 2022, during what became known as a *stealth* or *shadow mobilization*, the Russian government experimented with several ways to recruit volunteer contract soldiers for the war in Ukraine. At times, the MOD tried to recruit directly, posting on regional job boards for certain positions.[7] In May 2022, summonses began to be emailed to reservists to report to local

---

[2] "Russia Elevated Requirements for Conscript Health" ["В России повысили требования к здоровью призывников"], RIA News [РИА Новости], September 9, 2021.

[3] "Russian Duma Approves Bill Raising Age Limit for Military Personnel to 65," Radio Free Europe/Radio Liberty, May 25, 2022.

[4] "Putin Signs Law to Mobilize Russians Who Committed Serious Crimes—RIA," *Jerusalem Post*, November 4, 2022.

[5] "The State Duma Allowed the Mobilization of Those Convicted of Serious Crimes" ["Госдума разрешила мобилизацию судимых по тяжким статьям"], Radio Liberty [Радио Свобода], October 27, 2022.

[6] According to one mobilized soldier, "'I can't really call it "medical examination" per se. They just inspected my body and gave me a form to fill out. They just asked what kind of illness I've had, how I'm feeling now, if I had wounds or infections—and that was it. Everyone was treated irresponsibly like that.'" This soldier and the other conscripts were "given shooting practice twice . . . while superiors took photos of them" (Vasilyev, 2023).

[7] Yury Baranyuk, "Wanted: Contract Soldier. Good Pay. Bonus for Destroying Ukrainian Tanks," Radio Free Europe/Radio Liberty, June 10, 2022.

registration offices and others to ask for volunteers for Ukraine.[8] By July 2022, Russia announced that 85 "volunteer battalions" would be formed, one per federal region (which would have totaled 34,000 personnel, assuming 400 soldiers in each battalion).[9] Kremlin officials placed the responsibility to generate and supply these units on regional officials. Professional contract service was opened to any man, regardless of prior experience, to boost numbers.[10] Wage arrears among these volunteer units were said to be common according to anecdotal reports from volunteers. Some of the contracts were initially very short—only two months—and there were no standards for mental or physical health.[11] It is unclear how many volunteers signed up, but at any rate, 34,000 personnel were inadequate to replace the number of Russian casualties that had been sustained at the time. Kremlin officials announced a formal mobilization for 300,000 personnel in September 2022. In the same month, the ability for foreign citizens to gain Russian citizenship after 12 months of contract military service was introduced, reduced from a three-year service requirement.[12]

The Wagner PMC and the Russian military have both recruited volunteers from prisons since summer 2022, offering prisoners amnesty for their crimes after a six-month combat tour in Ukraine. More than 5,000 such amnesties had occurred for Wagner personnel alone by March 2023 according to its late founder, Yevgeny Prigozhin.[13] The MOD is offering 18-month

---

[8] "For the First Time Since March, the Russian Ministry of Defense Announced Casualties in Ukraine. The Figure Is Less Than the Known Names of the Dead" ["Минобороны России впервые с марта назвало потери в Украине. Цифра меньше, чем известно фамилий погибших"], BBC Russian Service [BBC Русская служба], September 21, 2022.

[9] Filip Bryjka, "Russia Recruiting Volunteers to Fight in Ukraine," Polish Institute of International Affairs, *PISM Bulletin*, Vol. 133, No. 2050, August 18, 2022.

[10] "'We Were Nothing to Them': Russian Volunteer Reservists Return from War Against Ukraine Feeling Deceived," Radio Free Europe/Radio Liberty, August 12, 2022.

[11] "'We Were Nothing to Them,'" 2022.

[12] Federal Assembly of the Russian Federation, "Foreign Citizens Serving in the Russian Army Under Contract to Be Able to Obtain Citizenship of Russia Under a Simplified Procedure," State Duma, September 20, 2022.

[13] "Prigozhin Says More Than 5,000 Former Prisoners Have Been Freed After Serving in Wagner Group," Meduza, March 26, 2023.

contracts to convicts in exchange for amnesty. Russia Behind Bars, a Russia-based NGO, estimates that more than 50,000 prisoners were recruited by both Wagner and the military as of early 2023.[14] By spring 2023, after several public spats between Prigozhin and Defense Minister Shoigu, Wagner was no longer allowed to recruit from prisons.

Russian President Vladimir Putin has said that conscripts will not serve in Ukraine, similar to announcements that he made during previous conflicts under his presidency. Despite some cases at the beginning of Russia's invasion, there is not much evidence to suggest that the military has broken this guidance and deployed conscripts to Ukraine.[15] It is more probable that conscripts are experiencing elevated pressure to convert to contract service during their conscription terms, given the military's manpower shortfalls and precedents for this coercive behavior prior to the 2014 invasion of Ukraine.[16] Russian NGOs note that coercion of conscripts is happening, that conscripts sign contracts under various conditions or threats, and that conscripts do not always understand their rights or what they signed up for.[17] Because of Shoigu's unrealistic goals of recruiting more than 400,000 contract service personnel in 2023, current conscripts are likely to face intense pressure to sign contracts.[18] When queried by the Russian media, the Eastern Military District's media office replied dryly that conscripts experiencing coercive practices should contact the military prosecutor's office and that "in each barracks there is an information stand with telephones, where a soldier can turn if he thinks his rights have been

---

[14] "Prigozhin Says More Than 5,000 Former Prisoners Have Been Freed," 2023.

[15] Bartles, 2019.

[16] Mills, 2015.

[17] Elena Pankratieva [Елена Панкратьева], "'Without Reading It, They Sign.' Committee of Soldiers' Mothers—About How 18-Year-Olds End Up in Military Service, and About Increasing Their Service Life" ["'Не вчитываясь, ставят подпись.' Комитет солдатских матерей—о том, как 18-летние попадают на СВО, и об увеличении срока службы"], Chita.RU [Чита.РУ], November 14, 2022.

[18] "Shoigu Proposed Increasing the Number of Military Personnel to 1.5 Million" ["Шойгу предложил увеличить численность военнослужащих до 1,5 млн"], RBC [РБК], December 21, 2022.

violated."[19] Soldiers often believe that these lines are monitored, so this suggestion is unlikely to be used.

Conscripts were an important part of the recruiting pipeline to contract service prior to the 2022 invasion according to previous RAND analysis.[20] Russia has attempted to expand this pool not only to meet annual draft requirements but also to enlist future contract service personnel. In July 2023, the Russian Duma expanded the draft age range from 18–27 to 18–30 years old and also prohibited travel outside Russia once conscription or mobilization notices are delivered.[21] By adding three years to the maximum draft age, the military will be able to expand the overall number of personnel by 2.3 million (not accounting for deferments or exemptions) based on Russian demographic trends reported by Rosstat, Russia's official statistics agency.[22] However, when factoring in the high rate of exemptions (75 percent of everyone who was called up for fall 2017, one of the last drafts with information on this point, received a deferment or an exemption), 2.3 million personnel will not go very far.[23] In the long run, Russia's population is likely to continue its decline in the 21st century. A 2019 United Nations assessment calculates Russia's population decline as anywhere from the current 146 million to 124 million or to an optimistic holding pattern of 147 million by 2050.[24]

---

[19] "Shoigu Proposed Increasing," 2022.

[20] Binnendijk et al., 2023.

[21] "Putin Signs Law Raising Maximum Draft Age," *Moscow Times*, August 4, 2023.

[22] Pavel Luzin, "New Draft and Mobilization Rules in Russia: Increased Coercion," *Eurasia Daily Monitor*, Vol. 20, No. 121, July 27, 2023.

[23] According to senior Russian military officials, 470,000 men were granted an exemption or deferment out of 623,000 called up for the fall 2017 draft. They also noted that 22 percent of those exemptions were because of health reasons or factors that otherwise rendered those men unfit for service ("More Than 470 Thousand People Received a Deferment or Exemption from the Army During the Autumn Conscription" ["Более 470 тыс. Человек получили отсрочку или освобождение от армии в ходе осеннего призыва"], TASS [ТАСС], January 11, 2017).

[24] "UN Predicts Russia's Population Could Halve by 2100," *Moscow Times*, June 18, 2019.

Expanding Tangible Benefits

In 18 months, the Russian government tried three methods to recruit additional volunteers to replace losses: two voluntary attempts and one based on mandatory mobilization. The first attempt was during summer 2022 with a recruiting campaign that offered increased wages and benefits. Some people were attracted to the money and the opportunity to serve.[25] When that effort failed to produce enough recruits to sustain Russia's occupied territories, the Kremlin ordered a partial mobilization of 300,000 in September 2022. By early 2023, the MOD announced unrealistic plans to expand the military's size and composition that included the return of multiple divisions and an increase in overall force size to 1.5 million. Also in 2023, Russian officials attempted a second all-volunteer enlistment campaign to bring in 400,000 additional volunteers. By December 2023, officials claimed to have recruited 490,000 into the military, a claim that is hard to corroborate.[26] In peacetime, it took six years to increase contract service personnel from 295,000 to 405,000 by 2020.[27]

During Russia's first volunteer recruiting drive in summer 2022, various benefits were offered to volunteers: 5,000–10,000 rubles per day combat pay, in addition to a base salary of 200,000 rubles per month.[28] This amount was almost four times the median national monthly average in Russia at the time.[29] State benefits, such as veteran status, health care, death benefits, and dependent benefits, were also offered. In the early phases of the recruit-

---

[25] According to one volunteer, "'I could be useful there.' 'And the money issue played a role. I thought I would pay off my debts and make a little something for my family.'" This same volunteer would provide a written refusal within a few weeks because of the conditions (Coalson, 2022).

[26] Kateryna Zakharchenko, "Russia Boosts Its Army with 'Voluntarily' Mobilized Students," *Kyiv Post*, December 20, 2023.

[27] Binnendijk et al., 2023.

[28] Mike Eckel, "'The Orchestra Needs Musicians': Behind the Covert Mobilization to Reinforce Russian Troops in Ukraine," Radio Free Europe/Radio Liberty, July 14, 2022; Orlova, 2022b.

[29] Trading Economics, "Russia Average Monthly Wages," database, undated.

ing drive, before mobilization, short-term contracts of two to three months were offered, but the practice quickly faded.[30]

Mobilized personnel in fall 2022 were reportedly offered similar incentives, and their jobs in Russia were notionally held for them while they were away fighting in Ukraine and their spouses protected from being laid off. When mobilization was announced in September, Russian lawmakers pushed through a series of laws that would pay mobilized personnel between 135,000 and 200,000 rubles per month as base pay depending on rank. Other benefits at the time included a debt repayment freeze while fighting and debt forgiveness in case of death.[31]

For Russia's spring 2023 all-volunteer recruiting call for 400,000, the Russian military again leaned into tangible benefits, offering flyers and posters that detailed the terms of contract service to fight in Ukraine and putting recruiting stations in well-trafficked locations. [32] Online advertisements also began surging in March 2023 on Russian social media—a 70 per-

---

[30] Eckel, 2022.

[31] Todd Prince, "Sweetening a Bitter Pill: Russia Offers Debt Breaks, Other Benefits to Entice Draftees," Radio Free Europe/Radio Liberty, September 28, 2022a.

[32] Binnendijk et al., 2023.

TABLE 3.1

Russian Ministry of Defense Contract Service Recruiting Benefits, Moscow, April 2023

Monetary Allowance[a]	Benefits	Russian Army Contract Service Social Guarantees
• Lump sum payment at contract signing – 195,000 rubles	• Guaranteed coverage of family's expenses	• High level of monetary allowance

• Payments before deployment to the SMO zone
  – Monetary allowance 40,000–50,000 rubles
  – Payment by decree of the Mayor of Moscow 50,000 rubles
	• School-age children
	  – Enrollment in any kindergarten (from 1.5 years)
	  – 200,000 rubles per year, two meals a day, after school care
		• Food security
		• Clothing security
		• Medical support
		• Acquisition of a specialty
		• Benefits for admission to universities

• Payments while deployed to the SMO zone
  – Monetary allowance (monthly base pay) 40,000–50,000 rubles
  – Additional combat pay 120,000–140,000 rubles (monthly)
  – Total 210,000–340,000 rubles for a full calendar month in the SMO zone
	• Elderly relatives 65 years and over
	  – 500,000 rubles per year—assistance of a social worker at home 3 times a week
	  – 1,000,000 rubles per year—accommodation at the elderly care center for health
	• Housing stipend
	  – 80,000 rubles annually
	• Next of kin
	  – Free training in selected professions at the best educational institutions
	• Additionally, 18,770 rubles per month per child
		• The right to receive additional education in military universities
		  – University admission benefits for you and your children
		• Free season passes to train in sports complexes of the MOD
		• Job retention for two years

SOURCE: Features information from Jonny Tickle [@jonnytickle], "This is the flyer they're handing out. According to this, soldiers fighting in the 'Special Military Operation Zone' receive a wage between 210k–340k rubles ($2,500–$4,200) a month," post on the X platform, April 7, 2023. Flyer translated by Dara Massicot.

[a] Payment amounts can vary depending on the duration of the contract, the territory of service, and changes in federal and regional regulations.

cent increase over 2020 levels according to *Novaya Gazeta Europe*.[33] These benefits would be robust if provided as described: The base pay remains high and a series of bonuses are promised. Social benefits for families are expanded to include benefits for elderly parents and admission to universities for the children of veterans. A full translation of the benefits, as of April 2023, derived from MOD recruiting materials is provided in Table 3.1.

The war in Ukraine has also revealed information about current Russian military salaries as of 2022. A recovered table of military salaries can be found in Table 3.2. Of note, the salaries for proxy commanders in Luhansk and Donetsk remained significantly less than their Russian military counterparts, while professional BARS reservist salaries were slightly higher.

TABLE 3.2

Monthly Russian, Proxy, and Reservist Base Pay Tables as of August 2022

Rank	Russian Armed Forces (rubles)	DNR/LNR Armed Forces (rubles)	BARS (rubles)
General-Major	318,049	224,000	X
Colonel	282,268	182,400	X
Lt. Colonel	266,578	166,400	270,000
Major	259,236	152,000	2XX,000 (illegible)
Captain	252,039	139,200	2XX,000 (illegible)
Sr. Lieutenant	241,730	131,200	2XX,000 (illegible)
Warrant officer	228,553	112,000	2XX,000 (illegible)
Sergeant	202,084	91,200	220,000
Soldier	187,551	76,800	205,000

SOURCE: Features information from Saito, Tsvetkova, and Zverev, 2022. Figures from Russian 11th Army Corps documents recovered from an abandoned headquarters in eastern Ukraine in August 2022. We assume this is the base monthly pay for these ranks. Some BARS pay was illegible because of damage to the recovered document. Translation by Clint Reach and Yuliya Shokh, RAND.

NOTE: DNR = Donetsk People's Republic; LNR = Luhansk People's Republic.

---

[33] Daria Talanova [Дарья Таланова] and Nikita Kondratyev [Никита Кондратьев], "Direct Outdoor to the Front" ["Прямая наружка на фронт"], *Novaya Gazeta Europe* [*Новой газеты Европа*], April 18, 2023.

Expanding Intangible Benefits

Russian officials have attempted to enhance the intangible benefits of military service since 2022 by using mixed media recruiting campaigns online, on television, and in print. There has also been a deliberate effort to link the war in Ukraine to the iconography and memory of WWII (called the *Great Patriotic War* in Russia) and to increase patriotic education in schools.

A review of recruiting commercials on television, online, and on posters or billboards in large cities and rural areas from summer 2022 to summer 2023 reveals common themes and insights into how and who officials are trying to recruit. Although not a comprehensive review of all available materials, these geographically diverse examples suggest that Russian officials are using themes of patriotism with a special focus on responsibility or obligation to defend the motherland and other themes that emphasize masculinity in particular. For example, the advertisements that make a direct appeal to masculinity convey messages that only "real men" serve in the military (for example, after implying that civilian jobs, such as taxi drivers, are inadequate, one 2023 commercial states that, "You're that real man [*Ti zhe muzhik*]. Be one." Or "Men, it's time").[34] These campaigns also denigrate those who have emigrated from Russia: One commercial stated directly, "Boys have left. But the men have stayed."[35] In another example in Moscow, a recruiting poster from early 2023 laid out the following list of intangible factors to entice people to service: "Russia: My history, my heroes, my soul, my country, my journey."[36] Other posters said simply, "My Profession is to Defend the Motherland" and "Join Your Own!"[37] Online advertisements used such phrases as "Contract service is the choice of real men!," "Military service is stability and confidence in life!," and "Your coun-

---

[34] NBC News, "Russian Military Encourages 'Real Men' to Step Forward in Recruitment Ad," video, YouTube, April 21, 2023; "Russia Expands War Recruitment Drive with Video Calling for 'Real' Men," NDTV, April 20, 2023.

[35] Ivan Doan, "'Boys Have Left, Men Have Stayed.' Best Russian Propagandist Cringe of the Year," video, YouTube, December 8, 2022.

[36] Farida Rustamova and Maxim Tovkaylo, "Anything but More Mobilization: Russia's Stealthy Push to Find More Soldiers," *Moscow Times*, April 6, 2023.

[37] "Russia Expands War Recruitment Drive," 2023; Newsman [@Taygainfo], post on Telegram, September 1, 2023.

try needs you!"[38] These concepts appear to be in line with prewar polling on patriotism and attitudes toward military service that were conducted by independent and state-controlled pollsters, from which top responses emphasized that "real men" join the military and that patriotism means love for country and a debt that is to be repaid when asked.[39]

In an attempt to bind current actions with the memories of past military glories, the Russian government has sought to link its 2022 invasion of Ukraine with WWII. The stated goal of Kremlin officials was to "denazify and demilitarize" Ukraine by falsely claiming that the Ukrainian government had been taken over by Nazism. The Russian government has also liberally used the iconography of WWII to link the two wars, such as by using the orange and black Saint George's ribbon pervasively in imagery about Russia's war in Ukraine. The Saint George's ribbon has been used since the early 2000s to commemorate military glory and remembrance of WWII.[40] Other direct links include WWII slogans ("Not One Step Back!") and, on Russian billboards, the use of iconic WWII Soviet photographs (such as Soviet troops on top of the Reichstag in 1945) placed side by side with Russian troops in Ukraine.[41]

Finally, previous RAND analysis noted an acceleration of patriotic education in Russia in the 2010s, particularly in schools that introduce the concept of military service at young ages and progressing through high school.[42] Since President Putin's public request in July 2022 to increase patriotic military education, the funding that has been allocated for this

---

[38] Talanova and Kondratyev, 2023.

[39] "Military Service Readiness and Hazing" ["Готовность к службе в армии и неуставные отношения"], VTsIOM [ВЦИОМ], December 21, 2020; "Military Threat" ["Военная Угроза"], Levada-Center [Левада-Центр], January 30, 2019.

[40] Andrei Dergalin, "St. George's Ribbon: Symbol of the Fight Against Nazism, Past and Present," Sputnik, April 25, 2023.

[41] Jade McGlynn [@DrJadeMcGlynn], "Moscow billboard: Images of Soviet WWII heroes montaged with images of modern-day Russian soldiers in Ukraine," post on the X platform, February 19, 2023.

[42] Binnendijk et al., 2023.

purpose has increased from $70 million in 2022 to $430 million in 2023.[43] The intensity and frequency of these initiatives has increased in schools and in social clubs since February 2022, from drills in school, such as competitions assembling rifles, to patriotic songs. These efforts are likely intended to militarize the youth and facilitate future recruitment.

These initiatives also have included the introduction of mandatory lessons that frame Russia's actions in Ukraine, visits to classrooms by Russian soldiers or veterans, an uptick in funding for patriotic camps for children, a patronage-like relationship between local military units and schools, patriotic media targeted at children, adjustments to school curriculums, and military arts and crafts in schools.[44] In July 2022, the Ministry of Education announced changes to school curriculums that include additional courses on "Russian Values."[45] In September 2022, a new program of mandatory classes called "Important Conversations" (which critics have called brainwashing sessions) was introduced, which frame the SMO in Kremlin-preferred terms and describe Russia's "struggle against the West." Students are threatened with expulsion if they do not attend.[46] In early 2023, Rozmolodezh, the federal agency for youth affairs, began an ill-advised program to send soldiers from the front who are on leave or who have been medically discharged to schools to speak about their experiences.[47] However, according to independent Russian media, these individuals have been affected by combat trauma and receive only four days of basic psychiatric support and youth mentorship training before visiting schools. The content of the discussions can

[43] Alla Hurska, "Generation Z: Russia's Militarization of Children," *Eurasia Daily Monitor*, Vol. 20, No. 134, August 18, 2023.

[44] Hurska, 2023.

[45] "Classes About the 'Values of Russian Society' Will Appear in Russian Schools" ["В российских школах появятся классные часы о 'ценностях российского общества'"], Mediazona [Медиазона], July 30, 2022.

[46] Alla Konstantinova, "'Teach Kids . . . So That They Are Proud of the War.' Russian School Children Threatened with Expulsion for Refusing to Attend 'Important Conversations,'" Mediazona, September 14, 2022.

[47] "'The Explosions Calm Them Down': What Russian Soldiers Are Teaching Children After Returning from the War in Ukraine," trans. by Emily ShawRuss, Meduza, April 26, 2023.

become graphic because some soldiers discuss combat or bring combat footage to show young children. A Russian psychologist who is familiar with the program noted that the content quickly can become traumatizing and that the program is being carried out without proper consideration for the children's psychological safety.[48] A group of teachers in one large Russian city resigned over these veteran "lessons," with one teacher saying that "many teachers understood that people who had returned from the war should not be allowed to [educate] children, as they might suffer from post-traumatic stress syndrome."[49]

Since war started, however, there are a few polls that suggest attitudes toward military service, mostly with respect to duty and patriotism, have hardened in two ways. Levada-Center polling from 2021 to mid-December 2022 indicated a slight shift in opinions on military service among all age groups. The most popular response in 2021 was that "every real man should serve in the Army" (a passive construct). During 2022, opinions started to shift and the response "military service is a duty that needs to be paid to the state no matter your personal views" (an active construct) became the most popular.[50] However, negative views of the military, such as "military service is senseless and should be avoided," increased among ages 18–24, 25–39, and 40–54, the populations that are eligible for mobilization. Negative views of the military decreased for the 55 and over age group for the first nine months after Russia's full-scale invasion—this group is beyond mobilization age (see Figure 3.1).

PMC recruiting drives also put tension on the military's wartime recruiting and retention efforts. The greatest recruiting competition that the Russian military faced was from the proliferation of PMCs after the war started,

---

[48] "'The Explosions Calm Them Down,'" 2023.

[49] Anastasia Tenisheva, "'Advocating for War Is Wrong': Russian Teachers Resign over Refusal to Allow Ukraine Veterans in Class," *Moscow Times*, September 7, 2023.

[50] For the December 2022 survey, the sample was made up of 1,601 people aged 18 or older from 137 municipalities in 50 regions of the Russian Federation. The survey was conducted as a personal interview in respondents' homes. The response distribution is given as a percentage of the total number of respondents, and the survey was conducted between November 24 and November 30, 2022 ("Military Conscription," 2021; "Russian Army," Levada-Center, December 16, 2022).

FIGURE 3.1

Russian Opinions on Military Service by Age

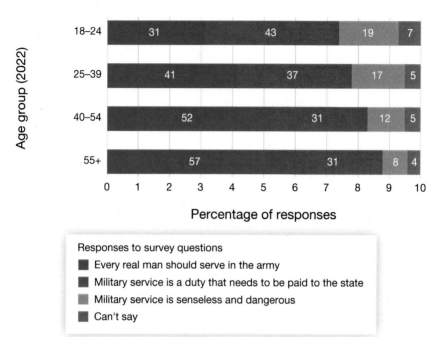

SOURCE: Adapted from "Russian Army," 2022. Respondents were asked, "What is your opinion on military service?" and then were asked to select a response from four choices. Possible responses were: "Every real man should serve in the army"; "Military service is a duty that needs to be paid to the state, no matter your personal views"; "Military service is senseless and dangerous and should be avoided at all costs"; and "Can't say."

although the matter was ultimately settled in the MOD's favor in July 2023, when all PMCs were made to sign contracts with the military.[51] The largest and most infamous Russian PMC in the Ukraine war was the Wagner Group. This was before the PMC was unofficially disbanded after its leaders rebelled in June 2023 and were subsequently killed in a plane crash in Russia

---

[51] Andrew Osborn, "Putin Backs Push for Mercenary Groups to Sign Contracts Despite Wagner's Refusal," Reuters, June 13, 2023.

in August 2023. British Defence Intelligence said that Wagner, at its height, maintained 50,000 fighters in Ukraine as of January 2023.[52]

In its recruiting commercials, Wagner tried to differentiate itself in terms of what it could compared with the military. Wagner offered short-term contracts and a base pay of 240,000 rubles per month, which is slightly higher than the military's base pay.[53] Wagner offered fewer social benefits than the military (it did not offer housing, dependent care, etc.) because of its PMC status.[54] The PMC effectively had two tiers of personnel: a trained tier that was recruited from the military, intelligence services, police, or Rosgvardia and an untrained tier that was recruited from prisons or from among people with no prior experience. The latter group was used as part of the human wave tactics that Wagner adopted in the Donbas and used extensively in the battle of Bakhmut.[55] In June 2022, Wagner recruiting ads used the following angles to claim that it was a more agile organization than the military:

> What does the company offer? A motivated, adult team with experienced fighters with extensive combat experience. The absence of an army madhouse, bureaucracy and other things. Constant real combat training, the opportunity to acquire new special skills. Opportunity to work all over the world.[56]

PMCs remain a competitor to the military for recruiting and retention, even if the MOD now controls them directly by contract. Young men who would otherwise be conscripted or recruited to contract service can instead enter into contracts with PMCs. Although these groups are at the Kremlin's

---

[52] Ministry of Defence [@DefenceHQ], "Latest Defence Intelligence update on the situation in Ukraine—20 January 2023. Find out more about the UK government's response: http://ow.ly/sUUI50MvNFH," post on the X platform, January 20, 2023a.

[53] Inna Sidorkova [Инна Сидоркова] and Alexander Atasuntsev [Александр Атасунцев], "Who and How Volunteers Are Recruited for Special Military Operations in Ukraine ["Кто и как набирает добровольцев на военную спецоперацию на Украине"], RBC [РБК], July 9, 2022.

[54] Sidorkova and Atasuntsev, 2022.

[55] "Bakhmut: Wagner Raises Russian Flag but Ukraine Fights On," BBC, April 3, 2023.

[56] Baranyuk, 2022.

disposal, there are no indications that PMC staffing counts against any official military billets. The available pool of recruits remains the same, which means that PMCs will continue to add pressure to military recruiters trying to make quotas.

Mobilization

Because Russia was unable to recruit enough volunteers to make up for losses that were sustained in spring and summer 2022, the Kremlin ordered a partial mobilization of 300,000 personnel in September 2022. As previous RAND analysis noted, Russia's mobilization base had largely been neglected for a decade because of other priorities and the belief that Russia would not fight a large, protracted land war in the near term.[57] Russia's mobilization system was ill-suited to respond to such a task with little preparation. The early mobilization was chaotic because each Russian region (*oblast*) was forced to meet quotas based on its population. Mistakes were made during the initial intake, such as mobilizing those with exemptions (e.g., having multiple young children, being single fathers, or having medial reasons). The initial waves of mobilized personnel received substandard training and equipment and were sent to Ukraine often with just a few days or a few weeks of training.[58] Mobilized personnel can range in age from 18 to 50 (and officers under 60).[59] Most are recruited from areas outside Moscow and Saint Petersburg. At a minimum, 347,000 military-aged males fled Russia to evade mobilization according to official statistics (200,000 fled to Kazakhstan, 69,000 fled to Georgia, 66,000 fled to European Union countries, and 12,000 fled to Mongolia). This number does not account for other destination countries that do not provide statistics on Russian emigration, so the overall number is likely to be higher than 347,000.[60] Another subtle indicator that certain parts of the Russian population have been attempting to evade military service is university enrollment; being a student counts as

---

[57] Charap et al., 2021.

[58] "Russia Sends Mobilized Men to Ukraine," 2022.

[59] Alisa Orlova, "Mobilization in Russia: Pertinent Details," *Kyiv Post*, September 21, 2022a.

[60] Nariman Gizitdinov and Helena Bedwell, "More Russians Flee Than Join Putin's Army After War Call-Up," Bloomberg, October 4, 2022.

a legal deferment under Russian conscription law. In 2022, 45,100 people entered postgraduate studies at Russian universities, the highest number in ten years (and more than 1.5 times 2021 levels, when 28,000 people were admitted).[61] Finally, there have been dozens of arson attempts at local military registration offices, signs of protest against mobilization. These acts of arson can be quite damaging because many records were kept on paper. As of early 2023, the Russian government is working to digitize those records.[62]

The families of the mobilized often advocate for those personnel to be better supplied and commanded through videos and other appeals to military prosecutor offices, governors, and President Putin. At times, the mobilized personnel themselves will make appeals using the same methods; between October 2022 and March 2023, mobilized personnel from at least 18 Russian regions made such appeals.[63] Many stories have emerged of mobilized personnel being trained initially as artillery specialists, as guards for facilities behind front lines, or as territorial defense forces.[64] This might have been the case originally because when mobilization was underway, Russian forces were settling into a defensive position in eastern and southern Ukraine. However, with the January 2023 appointment of General Gerasimov and the immediate shift to a winter offensive, mobilized soldiers were reclassified as infantry or "storm troops" and were ordered to directly assault Ukrainian positions, a decision that led to a high number of casualties.[65]

---

[61] Egor Gubernatorov [Егор Губернаторов,], "The Number of Graduate Students Admitted in 2022 Was the Highest in the Last 10 Years" ["Число принятых в 2022 году аспирантов стало максимальным за последние 10 лет"], Vedomosti [Ведомости], May 16, 2023.

[62] Olya Romashova, "'I Don't Know How Else to Get Through to Our Government': A Russian Arsonist Explains His Thinking," trans. by Sam Breazeale, Meduza, October 18, 2022.

[63] Layout [Вёрстка], Mobilized complaint [Мобилизованные жалуются], post on Telegram, March 9, 2023.

[64] "'Sent There to Be Meat': Why Russian Draftees Are Suddenly Publishing So Many Video Pleas to Putin," trans. by Sam Breazeale, Meduza, March 9, 2023.

[65] "'Sent There to Be Meat,'" 2023.

Wartime Retention Policies: Mobilization and Compelled Retention

Retention in the Russian military since the 2022 invasion of Ukraine is facing serious and mounting pressure. However, the effects of these retention problems have been masked since September 2022 when mobilization laws were introduced. The Russian government has used legislation to artificially retain personnel—which means that no contract enlisted personnel, officers, or mobilized personnel can resign or otherwise voluntarily leave service—so the true effect on retention as of September 2023 is unknown and will be revealed in full once restrictions are lifted.[66] In the meantime, the MOD is providing expanded wartime benefits, such as combat pay, other bonuses, and social benefits, to service personnel and their dependents. However, other factors that influence an individual's choice to remain in service have deteriorated sharply, such as order and discipline in units, combat conditions in Ukraine, and near continuous combat deployment with little rest.

Before I address retention failures, it should be noted that not all personnel will want to leave the military. For example, some personnel are attracted to the large sums of money and the promises of military housing or mortgage assistance.[67] According to intercepted phone calls and footage provided by the Ukrainian government, others are engaged in criminal activity, such as looting Ukrainian homes for civilian goods to send back to their relatives in Russia.[68] Some personnel wanted to resign when it was still possible in 2022 but felt they could not for financial reasons. The families of some personnel live in military-provided apartments,

---

[66] Sheftalovich, 2022.

[67] According to one Russian defector about his reasons for joining, "'A person who has some kind of income and financial assistance from his parents can choose where he, according to his personal convictions, goes to work. And for me, a person who lives with his mother on 27 square meters and wants to start his own family, wants to get out of the swamp of poverty, the choice is simple—go to work where they pay'" (Nikita Kondratyev [Никита Кондратьев], "'The Soldiers Looked at the Political Officer as a Savior and Went to Die'" ["'Солдаты смотрели на замполита как на спасителя и шли умирать'"], *Novaya Gazeta Europe* [*Новой газеты Европа*], February 28, 2023).

[68] Al-Hlou, Froliak, and Hill, 2022.

and leaving the military would have meant that their families would have nowhere to live. Or those families needed the housing stipend or bonus for upcoming purchases.[69]

Others did attempt to resign before September 2022, when it was still possible, but found that their commanding officers were either unavailable or unwilling to start the contract termination process.[70] Still other soldiers were deterred by penalties for refusing orders or for desertion. According to Russian personnel in Ukraine who make appeals to the Kremlin, there have been persistent accounts since 2022 that the Russian command is using barrier troops (blocking units to prevent desertions or unauthorized retreats) with orders to shoot those who leave their positions.[71] According to Russian social media accounts from soldiers and their families, those who refuse orders (*refuseniks*) are often detained in poor conditions (such as basements or jails) inside occupied Ukraine, where they are beaten or threatened with legal penalties by intelligence officers or political officers until they return to the front or are sent back to Russia.[72]

Since the September 2022 presidential decree authorizing mobilization, all personnel contracts have been extended indefinitely. This means that no officers, professional contract soldiers, or mobilized personnel have the ability to resign or otherwise voluntarily terminate contracts until the mobilization is ended.[73] Since the mobilization was announced, there are only three legal conditions for dismissal: being declared unfit for service, reaching the

---

[69] Nikita Solugub, "'I'm F---ing Done with This Army.' Russian Military Stunned as Mediazona Tells Them Their Secret Calls from Ukraine Published in the New York Times," Mediazona, March 17, 2023; Kinetz, 2023.

[70] Kondratyev, 2023.

[71] Kanal13, "Russian Soldiers Refuses to Comply with Command Order," video, YouTube, March 30, 2023; Pjotr Sauer, "Russian Soldiers Say Commanders Used 'Barrier Troops' to Stop Them Retreating," *The Guardian*, March 27, 2023.

[72] As an example of what refuseniks encounter, one soldier said that their commanding officers told them the following: "He called us dogs and said that we would be considered traitors at home. He said we'd 'be abandoned' and that our relatives would have 'no life'" (Coalson, 2022).

[73] Vkladka, 2023.

military service age limit, or being sentenced to prison.[74] Therefore, retention, for now, is compulsory.

As of May 2023, families of mobilized personnel have petitioned President Putin for mobilization term limits and have pointed to the short deployments of National Guard or Ministry of Internal Affairs units, which deploy for three to six months.[75] After large numbers of refusals following the disastrous opening weeks of the war, more than 1,000 National Guard personnel were rumored to have refused additional deployment to Ukraine. To avoid additional resignations in the National Guard, Russian officials modified the deployment policies: Now, only volunteers are deployed, and those that do deploy are kept in the rear of occupied Ukrainian areas, away from front lines.[76]

Increasing Benefits for Wartime Retention

Even though the Russian government has used legislation to artificially freeze retention since September 2022, it is attempting to stabilize future retention via policy changes. In 2023, the Russian government began offering a mixture of tangible benefits to service personnel in Ukraine and their families, including veterans' benefits. As discussed in Chapter 2, active service personnel are entitled to combat pay, death benefits, and other social benefits for their families. As of fall 2023, death benefits were around 12.5 million rubles ($166,000), plus benefits from regional governments of 1–3 million rubles ($17,000–$51,000).[77] Dependents of personnel who are classified as missing in action are not entitled to any compensation until the

---

[74] Pavlova, 2023.

[75] Baranyuk, 2022; Siberia.Realities [Сибирь.Реалии], "8,000 Relatives of Those Mobilized Signed a Petition Demanding That Time Limits Be Set for Their Men to Stay in the War in Ukraine" ["8000 родственников мобилизованных подписали петицию с требованием установить предельные сроки пребывания их мужчин на войне в Украине"], post on Telegram, May 5, 2023.

[76] Sevrinovsky, 2022.

[77] Todd Prince, "A Russian Father Left His Family Decades Ago. Now He Wants Half His Dead Son's Ukraine War Compensation," Radio Free Europe/Radio Liberty, November 11, 2022b; "Deceased Russian Soldier's Family Uses Compensation Payment to Buy New Car 'in His Memory,'" Meduza, July 18, 2022.

status is changed to missing in action–presumed killed or killed in action or a period of two years after the war ends.[78]

Mobilized personnel receive additional benefits and protections as well. In addition to their combat pay, mobilized personnel will receive full veterans' benefits at the end of the war, such as free public transport and health care, frozen loan repayments for themselves and their families while deployed, and protections to hold their civilian jobs while they are in Ukraine.[79] According to a working group established by the federal government, as of May 2023, mobilized personnel and others fighting in Ukraine will be eligible for the following benefits:

- 10 percent of Russian university admissions reserved for personnel who receive Heroes of Russia honors, personnel who hold three or more orders of courage, and all children of SMO veterans
- free legal assistance for veterans and their families
- television and video streaming capabilities for mobilized personnel and other soldiers to communicate with their families from Ukraine
- veterans' preference to apply to civil service jobs[80]
- proper rest and rotation for mobilized personnel to receive care and family time.[81]

This mobilized personnel working group also equalized pay for those deployed to Ukraine because some mobilized were making more money than active-duty contract service personnel.[82] The working group also proposed drafting laws to extend veteran status to proxy fighters in the

---

[78] Talanova and Asanova, 2023.

[79] "What Benefits Are Provided for SVO Participants? Graphic Arts" ("Какие льготы предусмотрены для участников СВО. Графика"], Izvestia [Известия], January 18, 2023.

[80] "Putin Promised Those Fighting in Ukraine Priority Hiring for Civil Service" ["Путин пообещал воюющим в Украине приоритетный наём на госслужбу"], *Moscow Times Russian Service*, February 21, 2023.

[81] President of Russia, "Meeting with First Deputy Speaker of the Federation Council Andrei Turchak," Presidential Executive Office, April 24, 2023.

[82] President of Russia, 2023.

Donetsk and Luhansk People's Republics and to create a federal standard of support for veterans if individual Russian regions cannot finance such care. Issues that remain unresolved as of May 2023 include transitioning from military care to civilian medical care as a veteran and expanding military mortgage assistance (reducing the amount of service time needed to receive full benefits).[83]

Attempts to Shape Impressions by Suppressing Bad News

Russian authorities are attempting to ensure domestic stability and to raise patriotism by suppressing negative information in the Russia media about the war and about service conditions. As already discussed, the retention of officers and contract service personnel was assisted prewar by improving service conditions and societal perceptions of military prestige. However, these factors have been disrupted for the overwhelming majority of personnel in the Ground Forces, VDV, Air Force, and Special Forces communities since Russia's 2022 full-scale invasion of Ukraine.[84] As summed up by one contract soldier reflecting on one year of war, "I heard someone say, 'Putin spent 20 years creating a professional contract army—then he pissed it away in a year. . . . Because it's not actually professional. It's all just on paper. . . .'"[85]

The Russian government has tried to shape perceptions of the war and to mask the extent of the damage to the military (both in terms of equipment and casualties) by offering incomplete information and by increasing penalties up to 15 years in prison for citizens or media sources that "discredit" the military.[86] Casualty figures are significantly underreported, and bad news (for example, the withdrawal from Kherson) is often rolled out through carefully orchestrated press events.[87]

Despite more than a decade of efforts to humanize the service and earn trust with military families, the Russian military is now undermining

---

[83] President of Russia, 2023.

[84] Binnendijk et al., 2023.

[85] Yapparova, 2023.

[86] "Putin Toughens Punishments for 'Discrediting' Russian Military," *Kyiv Independent*, March 18, 2023.

[87] NBC News, "Russian Defense Minister Announces Withdrawal of Troops from Kherson," video, YouTube, November 9, 2022.

those earlier efforts through a lack of compassion and information sharing. Multiple commanders have shown a certain callousness to the families of the missing or the deceased, a sad tradition that goes back decades. As an organization, the MOD treats many families of the wounded or killed as a nuisance or with contempt, habits that date to Soviet era–conflicts, such as those in Afghanistan, and through to Chechnya and the 2014 invasion of Ukraine.[88] In one particularly egregious example, the high-profile case of the sunk *Moskva* cruiser, the base commander shrugged in the face of a grieving father and told him his missing son was "somewhere at sea." The base commander was relieved only after the father and other relatives went public. Other *Moskva* relatives were stonewalled and treated with contempt when they called bases for updates on their children: "We don't need your hysterics here," one mother was told.[89]

Word about poor conditions and poor leadership is spreading through families and social networks, often with a message about warning others to avoid the military, although the data points are anecdotal and firm conclusions about the pervasiveness of this sentiment are unavailable. Families and soldiers record videos from many regions in Russia and make pleas for help to supply the soldiers and improve their chances for survival.[90] For example, contract soldiers fighting in Ukraine have expressed to their families that they do not want their children to join the military, which suggests a significant and lasting loss of trust that will carry far beyond this war's end for some affected families.[91] For others, ensuring their children never join

---

[88] Julie Elkner, "*Dedovshchina* and the Committee of Soldiers' Mothers Under Gorbachev," *Journal of Power Institutions in Post-Soviet Societies*, No. 1, 2004; Alec Luhn, "They Were Never There: Russia's Silence for Families of Troops Killed in Ukraine," *The Guardian*, January 19, 2015; Elizabeth Rubin, "'Only You Can Save Your Sons,'" *New York Times*, July 8, 2001.

[89] Alexey Slavin, "'What Does Missing in Action Mean? Is My Son Dead?' Meduza Talks to Mothers of Conscripts Who Served Aboard the Sunken Russian Warship Moskva," trans. by Eilish Hart, Meduza, April 20, 2022.

[90] According to one intercepted call between a soldier and his wife, "Vanya, the coffins keep arriving. We are burying one man after another. This is a nightmare. The wives are going crazy. They're even writing to Putin" (Al-Hlou, Froliak, and Hill, 2022).

[91] Said one solider in Ukraine, "'I'm f---ing quitting. I'm going to get a civilian job. And my son will not go to the army, I tell you one hundred percent. So, tell him that he will

the military is their final request. In one intercepted phone call, a soldier who believes his unit is being sent to their deaths relays a request to his wife for their son:

> You have to make sure he doesn't join the Army. . . . Ask Mom to get Uncle Gena involved to do everything within his power to make sure he doesn't join the Army. This will be my last . . . thing that I want.[92]

Veteran Care Issues: A Long-Term Retention Crisis

Casualties and combat trauma affected the Soviet and 1990s-era Russian military in significant and long-term ways, even when the deployed force was a much smaller percentage of the overall military. The large percentage of Russian forces deployed in Ukraine, particularly from the Ground Forces, VDV, and parts of the Air Force, will distinguish this operation from the Soviet failures in Afghanistan, Russia's wars in Chechnya and Georgia, and the 2014 invasion of Ukraine. No unit has been unaffected from casualties and combat stress. To compare the conflicts, an estimated 97 percent of all available Ground Forces and VDV units were fighting in Ukraine as of February 2023 according to estimates from the UK Ministry of Defence.[93] In Afghanistan, only 10 percent of all Soviet Ground Forces officers cycled through the conflict and only one formation from the Ground Forces—the Soviet 40th Combined Arms Army—was deployed.[94] The Russian military's force size in Chechnya varied from 40,000–100,000 personnel during its

---

be a doctor'" (Solugub, 2023).

[92] Security Service of Ukraine [Служба безпеки України], "The occupiers, who have sensed the strength of the ZSU, are preparing their dying laments for their loved ones" ["Окупанти, які відчули силу ЗСУ, готують передсмертні прохання своїм близьким"], post on Telegram, April 8, 2022.

[93] Isabel Coles and David Luhnow, "Russia Has Deployed 97% of Army in Ukraine but Is Struggling to Advance, U.K. Says," *Wall Street Journal*, February 15, 2023. Secretary of Defense Ben Wallace also said Russian forces' "combat effectiveness depleted by 40 percent, and nearly two-thirds of their tanks [were] destroyed or broken."

[94] The Soviet 40th Army increased to 81,000 personnel by 1980 and eventually reached 109,000 personnel when accounting for State Security Committee (KGB) and Ministry of Internal Affairs troops. During the second war in Chechnya, peak strength was estimated to be 100,000 Russian forces (Braithwaite, 2011, p. 126; Martin Malek,

wars there, but it was also heavily staffed by personnel from other organizations and not just the military.[95] Russia's 2014 invasion of Ukraine, with an estimated peak strength of 10,000 personnel in December 2014, was supported by a rotational force of 42,000 kept in the Southern Military District according to a 2015 Royal United Services Institute report.[96] These wars resulted in veterans who struggled to cope with re-adjusting to civilian life, which gave rise to such descriptors as "Afghan syndrome" (*Afgantsy*) or "Chechen syndrome." In more recent years, the phrase posttraumatic stress disorder (PTSD) has been imported from the West (Posttravmaticheskoe Stressovoye Rasstroistvo).

Anecdotes are emerging from the echoes of previous Russian wars that soldiers deployed to Ukraine are facing challenges getting proper medical care, both while in service and when medically discharged from the military. In some cases, personnel are being sent back to the front despite doctor recommendations for physical therapy for combat injuries or for psychiatric support for cases of severe mental health disorders from combat.[97] For personnel who receive medical discharges and convert to veteran status, some experience difficulties receiving care and accessing health entitlements.[98] Russian field medicine is under strain, which could contribute to more lifelong problems for veterans. For example, according to a Russian specialist in tactical medicine, "more than 30% of amputations were performed due to [the] incorrect application of a tourniquet" and "more than 50% of all deaths did not occur from life threatening injuries" but from poor care

---

"Russia's Asymmetric Wars in Chechnya Since 1994," *Connections*, Vol. 8, No. 4, Fall 2009).

[95] Olga Oliker, *Russia's Chechen Wars 1994–2000: Lessons from Urban Combat*, RAND Corporation, MR-1289-A, 2001.

[96] Igor Sutyagin, "Russian Forces in Ukraine," Royal United Services Institute for Defence and Security Studies, March 2015.

[97] "Wounded Russian Soldiers Returned to Front Without Proper Treatment— Agentstvo," *Moscow Times*, January 12, 2023.

[98] 76.ru—Yaroslavl online, "*The problem was solved for six months*" ["*Проблему решали полгода*"], post on Telegram, May 5, 2023.

in the field.[99] The same specialist noted that 90 percent of Russian combat wounds in Ukraine are from artillery shrapnel.[100]

Russian officials do not appear to be poised to provide adequate mental health care for soldiers and veterans, despite policy initiatives announced in 2023, which is likely to have a negative effect on retention and other social problems in Russia more broadly. As noted in a previous RAND report on PTSD, accessible care means that care is affordable, available, timely, perceived as acceptable or without stigma, and can accommodate the target population.[101] Providing this care could be challenging in Russia for a few structural reasons.

Although funding does not appear to be an issue at present, the shortage of psychiatrists trained for combat trauma in Russia is a challenge.[102] In addition, because of the Russian law that prohibits "disparaging the Armed Forces," an affected soldier and therapist might not feel comfortable being candid about the war in a therapy setting for many reasons.[103] Other issues facing veterans could include fear of sharing incriminating information about war crimes, fear that the information will be passed to the authorities or commanding officers, and shame from seeking therapy, which is not a common practice in Russian military culture. Russia has closed all but ten

---

[99] "Artem Katulin: The Ability to Provide First Aid Makes You Human" ["Артем Катулин: умение оказать первую помощь делает вас человеком"], RIA News [РИА Новости], April 27, 2023.

[100] The specialist went on to say that "most fighters" try to crowdsource or build their own medical kits to supplement the official Russian military kit, which, according to him, was 75 percent Chinese components. Only in spring 2023 was a new medical kit introduced ("Artem Katulin," 2023).

[101] Carrie M. Farmer and Lu Dong, *Defining High-Quality Care for Posttraumatic Stress Disorder and Mild Traumatic Brain Injury: Proposed Definition and Next Steps for the Veteran Wellness Alliance*, RAND Corporation, RR-A337-1, 2020, citing Roy Penchansky and J. William Thomas, "The Concept of Access: Definition and Relationship to Consumer Satisfaction," *Medical Care*, Vol. 19, No. 2, February 1981.

[102] Natalia Kostarnova [Наталья Костарнова], "Posttraumatic Stress Disorder" ["Посттравматическое стрессовое устройство"], Kommersant [Коммерсантъ], March 19, 2023.

[103] Anna Ryzhkova, "'He Survived War but Not Rehabilitation': An Employee at a Rehab Center Describes Caring for Russian Soldiers Returning from the Front," trans. by Emily Laskin, Meduza, March 18, 2023.

of its military psychiatric institutions since the 1990s, and only one of those institutions has a center for physical and psychological rehabilitation, with only 32 beds according to Russian veterans' rights groups.[104]

Excess personnel who experience debilitating combat trauma are sent to military sanatoriums, which in Russia are vacation sites, and many provide on-site health care for active-duty personnel and veterans.[105] A few of these sanatoriums have basic psychiatric clinics and physical therapy support, but they are insufficient for the specialized types of care that are needed according to one of the workers. If there are amputees or severely wounded soldiers, the sanatoriums do not have the staff to care for them, and the soldiers' mothers typically come to care for them.[106] The mixing of vacationers and soldiers with severe combat stress is not going well; according to one of the sanitorium workers, the vacationers disapprove of the disruption to their retreat from mentally distressed soldiers, or the injured young men make the vacationers fearful about their own children being drafted.[107] In any case, the sanatoriums do not have sufficient staff to treat the soldiers' mental distress, and some soldiers purchase alcohol off-site, retreat to their rooms, and drink alone.

Russian officials seem to be taking some steps to cope with the return of soldiers who have physical or mental combat traumas. As a result of the wars in Afghanistan and Chechnya, there is a basis of understanding of PTSD and several universities, medical associations, and veterans groups that maintain professional knowledge for treatment and new treatment techniques.[108] Some of these professionals acknowledge that, historically, between 20–25 percent of combat participants are affected by PTSD.[109]

---

[104] Kostarnova, 2023.

[105] Ryzhkova, 2023.

[106] Ryzhkova, 2023.

[107] Ryzhkova, 2023.

[108] Kostarnova, 2023; Polina Tiunova [Полина Тиунова], "In Chelyabinsk, Doctors Gave Advice on How the Military Can Cope with the Consequences of Combat Psychological Trauma," ["В Челябинске врачи дали советы, как военным справиться с последствиями боевой психологической травмы"], Bezformata [Безформата], October 13, 2022.

[109] Tiunova, 2022.

Another professional believes that 100,000 personnel will need professional medical help when they return from the war in Ukraine.[110] Therefore, the challenge seems to be one of capacity. Russian officials announced the creation of a pilot program in March 2023 (one year after the start of the war) to treat PTSD, but this program comes too late for many soldiers who are already affected.[111] Furthermore, President Putin in spring 2023 authorized a federal program called the Defenders of the Fatherland Fund, which aims to create at least one support center for returning veterans in each federal region. These facilities are intended to provide physical rehabilitation and therapy, mental health care, and legal and employment assistance and to help veterans navigate their benefits.[112] The government also created a new holiday—July 1 is now the day of Combat Veterans.[113]

As it stands as of this writing, the experiences of the few personnel who have returned suggest that the care has been unhelpful. Some returned soldiers are turning to drinking to avoid nightmares about the war, while others are returning to the combat zone thinking it will bring them relief from their struggles to reacclimate to civilian life.[114] Eventually, a large population of troubled veterans could negatively affect public perception of the Russian military, particularly if veterans from Ukraine fail to adapt and fall into crime, unemployment, or poverty, as was the case in the 1990s. In the

---

[110] Sergey Valchenko [Сергей Вальченко], "The Expert Warned About Possible Psychological Problems of Veterans of the SVO" ["Эксперт предупредила о возможных психологических проблемах участников СВО"], Moskovsky Komsomolets [Московский Комсомолец], December 2, 2022.

[111] Ilya Lakstygal [Илья Лакстыгал] and Anastasia Mayer [Анастасия Майер], "The Program of Psychological Assistance to Veterans of the Special Operation Is Planned to Be Expanded" ["Программу психологической помощи участникам спецоперации планируют расширить"], Vedemosti [Ведомости], March 20, 2023.

[112] V. Putin [В. Путин], "On the Creation of the State Fund for Supporting Participants in the Special Military Operation 'Defenders of the Fatherland'" ["О Создании Государственного Фонда Поддержки Участников Специальной Военной Операции 'Защитники Отечества'"], Decree of the President of the Russian Federation [Указ Президента Российской Федерации], *Guardian of the Baltic* [*Страж Балтики*], Vol. 12, April 7, 2023.

[113] President of Russia, 2023.

[114] "'I Go to War in My Sleep,'" 2023.

1990s, veterans from Afghanistan were called, often with suspicion or pity, *Afghantsy*, and veterans from Chechnya were viewed in similar ways.[115] A Russian therapist who has worked with soldiers who have fought in Ukraine since 2022 is sounding the alarm about the wave of PTSD-affected veterans who will eventually return home to insufficient support:

> These kinds of people will lose their jobs, because they'll curse out their bosses and hit them," he said. "They'll lose their families, and they'll lose their freedom, because if a police officer gets near them, they'll punch him in the head. How many guys fell into crime after Afghanistan? If we don't have a well-thought-out plan for rehabilitating soldiers, it will spell the end of civil society.[116]

Conclusions for Recruiting and Retention

Since the start of the war in 2022, Russian officials have attempted on three different occasions to expand recruiting to account for personnel losses and to hold occupied territory. The first attempt in summer 2022 was voluntary and relied on expanding tangible benefits, such as more-competitive combat pay and social benefits, and making intangible appeals to patriotism. However, these enticements were insufficient to attract the required numbers of personnel to the war effort. This disparity suggests that there are other tangible and intangible factors about the war in Ukraine that outweighed these enticements and suppressed willingness to join the war effort, such as the risk of injury or death from combat, rumors of casualties and the suppression of those facts by authorities, communications from soldiers to their families and friends about bad commanders, and the lack of supplies. The Russian military's conduct of the war, heavy casualties, and the mistreatment of its personnel are likely outweighing the tangible benefits that are being offered, at least while the active phase of the war is underway.

Russian authorities were forced to order a partial mobilization in fall 2022 when volunteer recruiting efforts failed, their second recruiting effort.

---

[115] Yana Petrova [Яна Петрова], "PTSD After the War in Chechnya" ["ПТСР после войны в Чечне"], Pikabu [Пикабу], July 1, 2021.

[116] "'I Go to War in My Sleep,'" 2023.

The third recruiting effort, which started in spring 2023, has attempted to attract 400,000 additional contract service personnel by December 2023. This ambitious goal announced by Defense Minister Shoigu seems highly unrealistic without coercion or another round of mobilization, based on previous years' recruiting rates.

However, it is worth noting that the effects on future recruiting are potentially not as dire if the war settles into a frozen conflict and casualties decline, and much will be contingent on the nature of the conflict resolution. As of spring 2023, Russia's leadership has signaled that it is willing to fund significant and tangible enticements for military service that could keep recruiting numbers relatively stable. Intangible factors, such as calls to patriotism and mandatory patriotic education, could also aid in future recruiting, particularly when the active phase of the war subsides. As reported in a previous RAND study, material benefits can be a powerful recruiting tool, at least in peacetime, when the stakes are lower for potential recruits.[117] Assuming that the Russian government is able and willing to provide the necessary resources to offer the competitive material benefits of pay, housing, and other supports, recruiting could stabilize after the active phase of the war is over.

Existing military retention problems are masked by mobilization and compulsory retention: All personnel who are deployed to Ukraine have been prohibited from terminating their contracts since mobilization was declared in September 2022. The Russian government continues to offer several tangible benefits packages to recruits and increased benefits for those already in service, such as combat pay and social guarantees. However, it remains to be seen whether those efforts will be sufficient when restrictions are eased and personnel are allowed to leave military service.

Tangible benefits were not enough to outweigh intangible factors for recruiting, such as risk, safety, and poor service conditions in Ukraine, so it stands to reason that similar dynamics could be at play when it comes to long-term retention. The military's uneven ability to provide accurate and on-time wages and health benefits to active-duty, mobilized, and medically discharged personnel is also likely to undermine retention because it shows

---

[117] Binnendijk et al., 2023.

that a key tangible benefit is likely to be difficult to obtain. The negative information that is spreading through families and social networks about the military (for example, poor tactics, high numbers of casualties, disillusionment, lack of trust up and down the command chain) stands in stark contrast to the incomplete and heavily distorted information that is provided by Russian authorities. The intangible benefits of military service, such as social trust and prestige that are tied to modern equipment and stable service conditions, are likely to be significantly affected.

As noted in a previous RAND report on this topic, the factors with the most impact on Russian military retention prior to the 2022 full-scale invasion of Ukraine were (1) the perception of good order and discipline and perceptions of well-being, (2) improved service conditions in the military, and (3) patriotism and broader public perceptions of military service.[118] Two of three of these intangible factors have been significantly disrupted as a result of the war in Ukraine: (1) good order and discipline and (2) improved service conditions. After the active phase of the war ends, it is more likely than not that retention will be significantly affected, as confidence in the military continues to degrade and as personnel are killed, are medically discharged, or are eligible for resignation. Only when wartime personnel restrictions are lifted will the true extent of the damage to Russian military prestige, social standing, and future recruiting and retention be seen.

For the third factor, the Russian government is trying to increase patriotism at home and to distract from personnel losses and the military's decline in prestige through various efforts, such as linking the conflict to the sacrifices made during WWII. Patriotism could remain steady in a generalized sense throughout the Russian population because of the government's intense efforts to repackage the war as an existential fight and to co-opt the historical memory of WWII and its participants as liberators or heroes. It remains to be seen whether those efforts will be successful at retaining personnel.

---

[118] Binnendijk et al., 2023.

CHAPTER 4

Implications for Future Military Manpower

The damage to the Russian military as a result of the losses it has sustained in its full-scale invasion of Ukraine is severe and will likely lead to several challenges for recruiting and retention in the years ahead. This analysis has identified several efforts that the Russian government is pursuing to stabilize wartime recruiting and retention. However, the heavy casualties, faltering offensives, poor force employment, and flawed unit leadership that soldiers are experiencing firsthand will undermine these efforts. The future makeup of Russia's military hangs in the balance. If the recruiting and retention of officers and professional enlisted personnel face severe disruptions in the years after the war, the Russian government could be forced to turn to socially unpalatable options, such as increasing the size of the conscription pool and lengthening conscription service terms, if it remains committed to a 1.5–million-man military in the face of worsening demographics. The key findings are as follows.

In the 18 months since Russia's full-scale invasion of Ukraine, intangible factors, such as the risk of injury or death, the breakdown of order and discipline, and poor conditions, appear to be outweighing the many tangible incentives that are being offered by the Russian government to stabilize recruiting and retention. For example, incentives for recruits and expanded benefits for active personnel in 2022 were robust but, ultimately, failed because rumors of casualties, the suppression of facts by the authorities, and communications from soldiers to their families and friends about bad commanders and the lack of supplies proliferated. An insufficient number of Russian men enlisted and many outright emigrated, which forced the Russian military to rely on mobilization to fill urgent manpower shortfalls.

Severe casualties and a brutal command style in Ukraine are threatening to undo 15 years of effort to create a more professional force. The full scale of the war's effects on retention were not yet known at the time of writing, but many of the pillars that contributed to successful retention prior to 2022 are at risk of severe disruption, which would leave the Russian government with only the option of heavily managing public perceptions of the war.

Recruiting could be less affected after the active phase of the war concludes if Russian authorities can maintain competitive material benefits. The Russian government is offering expanded tangible benefits, such as combat pay that is well above the national average and other bonuses, housing benefits, and lifelong medical care, to aid recruiting and retention as of 2023. For some, these benefits are attractive, particularly if they can be maintained following the active phase of the war and could assist with recruiting and retention in the future. After the active phase of the war concludes and casualties decline, if Russian authorities continue to offer the competitive tangible benefits of high salaries and social benefits, it might be able to recruit personnel who are enticed by these economic considerations. Much will depend on how the conflict ends, whether that resolution is viewed as successful, and the political outcomes in Russia.

Future retention rates are unknown because, since the September 2022 mobilization, no one can voluntarily leave service. Retention has been frozen since the Kremlin issued an edict in September 2022 that prohibits military personnel from terminating their contracts until the government declares the SMO over. The war's effects on retention within the Ground Forces, VDV, and Special Forces are currently masked but could be severe when the restrictions are rescinded.

The Russian government is actively trying to manipulate domestic impressions of the war and of military performance. The government is using intangible factors to increase feelings of patriotism and duty and progressively framing the war in Ukraine as an existential conflict against the West. The Russian government suppresses negative information about combat casualties and poor performance using various means, such as changes to the legal code and arrests. The increase in military–patriotic education in schools in the years prior to 2022, and especially after the full-scale invasion, suggests that Russian authorities are trying to shape the next generation of recruits and their families.

Structural factors and political officers could be partially to blame for widespread Russian war crimes and other atrocities in occupied Ukraine. Russian political officers, who are supposed to ensure loyalty, patriotism, and compliance with the laws of war, do not appear to be effective at these tasks, despite being present at multiple levels of command within Russian Ground Forces units in Ukraine. As a result of how the Russian military structures its command within the units, no single unit commander feels accountable for the war crimes committed by their subordinates: Ensuring adherence to the laws of war and training troops about that conduct are tasks that have fallen to the political officer, a deputy unit commander who often does not have command authority.

Russian authorities are not postured to adequately cope with large numbers of casualties or, in particular, the invisible wounds of returning veteran PTSD. Programs offering assistance were created in spring 2023 but, at the time of this writing, there were an insufficient number of facilities and trained therapists to support veterans in crisis in Russia, and one large-scale federal program on the books, the Defenders of the Fatherland fund, is insufficiently resourced.

The Russian military's future personnel needs will vary by rank. Many young professional contract service personnel and junior officers have been killed or wounded in Ukraine. As of September 2023, Russia's losses outpaced a decade of war in Afghanistan and a decade of war in Chechnya according to multiple non-Russian sources because Russia almost certainly continues to underreport deaths.

Abbreviations

AWOL	absent without leave
BARS	Boevoy Armeyskiy Rezerv Strany (Special Combat Army Reserve)
BTG	battalion tactical group
FSB	Federal Security Service
MOD	Ministry of Defense
NCO	noncommissioned officer
NGO	nongovernmental organization
PMC	private military company
PTSD	posttraumatic stress disorder
SMO	special military operation
UAF	Ukrainian Armed Forces
VDV	Airborne Forces

References

Unless otherwise indicated, the authors of this report provided the translations of bibliographic details for the non-English sources included in this report. To support conventions for alphabetizing, sources in Russian are introduced with and organized according to their English translations.

11th Army Corps, "Combat and Personnel Composition of the Balakiliia Force Grouping as of August 2022," trans. by Clinton Reach and Yuliya Shokh, September 2022.

76.ru—Yaroslavl online, *The problem was solved for six months* [*"Проблему решали полгода"*], post on Telegram, May 5, 2023. As of August 5, 2023: https://t.me/news76/25752

Alexievich, Svetlana, *Boys in Zinc*, Penguin Books, 2017.

Al-Hlou, Yousur, Masha Froliak, and Evan Hill, "'Putin Is a Fool': Intercepted Calls Reveal Russian Army in Disarray," *New York Times*, audio trans. by Aleksandra Koroleva and Oksana Nesterenko, September 28, 2022.

Arenina, Katya [Аренина, Катя], "'I Would Then Be Missing in Action': How and Why Contract Soldiers Flee the Russian Army" ["'Был бы потом без вести пропавшим': Как и почему контрактники бегут из российской армии"], Important Stories [Важные истории], October 29, 2020.

"Artem Katulin: The Ability to Provide First Aid Makes You Human" ["Артем Катулин: умение оказать первую помощь делает вас человеком"], RIA News [РИА Новости], April 27, 2023.

Asch, Beth J., *Setting Military Compensation to Support Recruitment, Retention, and Performance*, RAND Corporation, RR-3197-A, 2019. As of December 6, 2023: https://www.rand.org/pubs/research_reports/RR3197.html

"Bakhmut: Wagner Raises Russian Flag but Ukraine Fights On," BBC, April 3, 2023.

Barabanov, Ilya [Барабанов, Илья], "'If They Put Me on a Combat Helicopter, I Would Have to Kill.' VKS Pilot Escaped from Russia and Spoke to the BBC" ["'Если бы меня посадили на боевой вертолет, мнебы пришлось убивать.' Пилот ВКС сбежал изРоссии и поговорил с Би-би-си"], BBC Russian Service [Русская служба Би-би-си], June 8, 2023.

Baranyuk, Yury, "Wanted: Contract Soldier. Good Pay. Bonus for Destroying Ukrainian Tanks," Radio Free Europe/Radio Liberty, June 10, 2022.

Bartles, Charles K., "Russian Armed Forces: Enlisted Professionals," *NCO Journal*, March 2019.

Binnendijk, Anika, Dara Massicot, Anthony Atler, John J. Drennan, Khrystyna Holynska, Katya Migacheva, Marek N. Posard, and Yuliya Shokh, *Russian Military Personnel Policy and Proficiency: Reforms and Trends, 1991–2021*, RAND Corporation, RR-A1233-6, 2023. As of November 30, 2023: https://www.rand.org/pubs/research_reports/RRA1233-6.html

Braithwaite, Rodric, *Afgantsy: The Russians in Afghanistan 1979–89*, Oxford University Press, 2011.

Bronk, Justin, *Russian Combat Air Strengths and Limitations: Lessons from Ukraine*, Center for Naval Analyses, April 2023.

Bryjka, Filip, "Russia Recruiting Volunteers to Fight in Ukraine," Polish Institute of International Affairs, *PISM Bulletin*, Vol. 133, No. 2050, August 18, 2022.

Bruntalsky, P. [Брунтальский, П.], "The Soldier Has a Day Off . . . Saturday and Sunday" ["У солдата выходной . . . Суббота и воскресенье"], *Military Industrial Courier* [*Военно-промышленный курьер*], No. 20, 2010.

Bychenko, Yu. G. [Быченко, Ю. Г.], and T. M. Balandina [Т. М. Баландина], "Development of the Professional Potential of Military Personnel Who Entered Military Service Under a Contract" ["Развитие профессионального потенциала военнослужащих, поступивших на военную службу по контракту"], *Bulletin of Nizhny Novgorod University* [*Вестник Нижегородского университета*], Vol. 4, No. 56, 2019.

Charap, Samuel, Dara Massicot, Miranda Priebe, Alyssa Demus, Clint Reach, Mark Stalczynski, Eugeniu Han, and Lynn E. Davis, *Russian Grand Strategy: Rhetoric and Reality*, RAND Corporation, RR-4238-A, 2021. As of December 1, 2023: https://www.rand.org/pubs/research_reports/RR4238.html

Cheianov, V., Esq. [@cheianov], "Captured Russian army field rations," post on the X platform, February 28, 2022. As of April 4, 2023: https://twitter.com/cheianov/status/1498414144579588102

CIT (en) [@CITeam_en], "This rare video was filmed by a (non-captured) Russian soldier complaining about losses and harsh conditions," post on the X platform, March 3, 2022. As of March 15, 2023: https://twitter.com/CITeam_en/status/1499361692261756945

"Classes About the 'Values of Russian Society' Will Appear in Russian Schools" ["В российских школах появятся классные часы о 'ценностях российского общества'"], Mediazona [Медиазона], July 30, 2022.

Coalson, Robert, "'I Didn't Think I'd Survive': Russian Volunteer Soldier Who Quit Ukraine War Recalls His Ordeal," Radio Free Europe/Radio Liberty, November 9, 2022.

Coles, Isabel, and David Luhnow, "Russia Has Deployed 97% of Army in Ukraine but Is Struggling to Advance, U.K. Says," *Wall Street Journal*, February 15, 2023.

"Conscripts Were Offered Permission to Conclude a Contract with the FSB" ["Военнослужащим-срочникам предложили разрешить заключать контракт с ФСБ"], RIA News [РИА Новости], November 1, 2021.

Cooper, Helene, Thomas Gibbons-Neff, Eric Schmitt, and Julian E. Barnes, "Troop Deaths and Injuries in Ukraine War Near 500,000, U.S. Officials Say," *New York Times*, August 18, 2023.

Crane, Keith, Olga Oliker, and Brian Nichiporuk, *Trends in Russia's Armed Forces: An Overview of Budgets and Capabilities*, RAND Corporation, RR-2573-A, 2019. As of August 29, 2022: rand.org/pubs/research_reports/RR2573.html

Cranny-Evans, Sam, "Understanding Russia's Mobilization," Royal United Services Institute for Defence and Security Studies, September 28, 2022.

Cranny-Evans, Sam, and Sidharth Kaushal, "Not Out of the Woods Yet: Assessing the Operational Situation in Ukraine," Royal United Services Institute for Defence and Security Studies, March 14, 2022.

"Deceased Russian Soldier's Family Uses Compensation Payment to Buy New Car 'in His Memory,'" Meduza, July 18, 2022.

Dergalin, Andrei, "St. George's Ribbon: Symbol of the Fight Against Nazism, Past and Present," Sputnik, April 25, 2023.

Doan, Ivan, "'Boys Have Left, Men Have Stayed.' Best Russian Propagandist Cringe of the Year," video, YouTube, December 8, 2022. As of December 1, 2023: https://www.youtube.com/watch?v=mW6XOP1I_eM

Douglas, Nadja, "Civil–Military Relations in Russia: Conscript vs. Contract Army, or How Ideas Prevail Against Functional Demands," *Journal of Slavic Military Studies*, Vol. 27, No. 4, 2014.

"Draftees from Irkutsk Appeal to Putin for Help: 'Command Told Us Directly That We Are Expendable,'" Meduza, February 26, 2023.

Dyachenko, A. N. [Дяченко, А. Н.], and V. N. Kozlov [В. Н. Козлов], "Hazing in the Russian Army as a Factor of Evasion from Military Service" ["Неуставные отношения в Российской армии как фактор уклонения от военной службы"], *Oboznik* [*Обозник*], October 2, 2018.

Eckel, Mike, "'The Orchestra Needs Musicians': Behind the Covert Mobilization to Reinforce Russian Troops in Ukraine," Radio Free Europe/Radio Liberty, July 14, 2022.

Elkner, Julie, "*Dedovshchina* and the Committee of Soldiers' Mothers Under Gorbachev," *Journal of Power Institutions in Post-Soviet Societies*, No. 1, 2004.

Encyclopedia of the Strategic Missile Forces [Энциклопедия РВСН], "Combat Capacity" [БОЕВАЯ СПОСОБНОСТЬ], webpage, 2013. As of April 4, 2023:
https://rvsn.academic.ru/2313/БОЕВАЯ_СПОСОБНОСТЬ

Ermolov, N. A. [Ермолов, Н. А.], and E. N. Karlova [Е. Н. Карлова], "Motivation for Military Service as a Subject of Theoretical and Empirical Research in Military Sociology" ["Мотивация к военной службе как предмет теоретических и эмпирических исследований в военной социологии"], *Academy* [*Академия*], Vol. 1, No. 28, 2018.

"'The Explosions Calm Them Down': What Russian Soldiers Are Teaching Children After Returning from the War in Ukraine," trans. by Emily ShawRuss, Meduza, April 26, 2023.

Farmer, Carrie M., and Lu Dong, *Defining High-Quality Care for Posttraumatic Stress Disorder and Mild Traumatic Brain Injury: Proposed Definition and Next Steps for the Veteran Wellness Alliance*, RAND Corporation, RR-A337-1, 2020. As of May 15, 2022:
https://www.rand.org/pubs/research_reports/RRA337-1.html

Federal Assembly of the Russian Federation, "Foreign Citizens Serving in the Russian Army Under Contract to Be Able to Obtain Citizenship of Russia Under a Simplified Procedure," State Duma, September 20, 2022.

"For the First Time Since March, the Russian Ministry of Defense Announced Casualties in Ukraine. The Figure Is Less Than the Known Names of the Dead" ["Минобороны России впервые с марта назвало потери в Украине. Цифра меньше, чем известно фамилий погибших"], BBC Russian Service [BBC Русская служба], September 21, 2022.

Garamone, Jim, "Russian Forces Invading Ukraine Suffer Low Morale," U.S. Department of Defense, March 23, 2022.

Gavrilov, Yuri [Гаврилов, Юрий], "Spring Recruitment into the Army Has Begun. 135 Thousand People Will Become Soldiers" ["Начался весенний набор в армию. Солдатами станут 135 тысяч человек"], *Rossiyskaya Gazeta* [*Российской газеты*], March 31, 2019.

"The General Staff Explained How the Ban on Smartphones for Conscripts Works" ["В Генштабе объяснили, как работает запрет на смартфоны для призывников"], RBC [РБК], March 31, 2021.

Gerashchenko, Anton, "Part 195. 'I Thought They Would Pay, but Damn'" ["Часть 195. 'Думал будут платить, а нихера'"], video, YouTube, April 13, 2022. As of March 5, 2023:
https://www.youtube.com/watch?v=I7nYrKD6gmI&t=12s

Gerasimov, V. V. [Герасимов, В. В.], "On the Progress of Executing the Directives of the President of the Russian Federation from 7 May 2012, Nos. 603, 604 and Development of the Armed Forces of the Russian Federation" ["О ходе выполнения указов Президента Российской Федерации от 7 мая 2012 года N603, 604 и развития Вооруженных Сил Российской Федерации"], *Military Thought* [*Военная мысль*], No. 12, 2017.

"Gives Us a Winning Point" ["дает нам победное очко"], Weapons of Russia [Оружие России], October 19, 2019.

Gizitdinov, Nariman, and Helena Bedwell, "More Russians Flee Than Join Putin's Army After War Call-Up," Bloomberg, October 4, 2022.

Goncharov, S. V. [Гончаров, С. В.], and B. B. Ostroverkhiy [В. В. Островерхий], "Assessment and Accounting by the Commander of a Formation (Military Unit) of the Socio-Political Situation in the Area of Upcoming Hostilities" ["Оценка И Учет Командиром Соединения (Воинской Части) Социально-Политической Обстановки В Районе Предстоящих Боевых Действий"], *Military Thought* [*Военная мысль*], No. 8, August 2021.

Goncharov, S. V. [Гончаров, С. В.], and O. G. Zaets [О. Г. Заец], "Assessment and Accounting of the Moral and Psychological Factor When Commanders Make Decisions Using Automated Troop Control Systems" ["Оценка и учет морально-психологического фактора при принятии командирами решений с использованием автоматизированных систем управления войсками"], *Military Thought* [*Военная мысль*], No. 8, 2015.

Grau, Lester W., and Charles K. Bartles, "Getting to Know the Russian Battalion Tactical Group," Royal United Services Institute for Defence and Security Studies, April 14, 2022.

Gresh, Jason P., "The Realities of Russian Military Conscription," *Journal of Slavic Military Studies*, Vol. 24, No. 2, 2011.

Gubernatorov, Egor [Губернаторов, Егор], "The Number of Graduate Students Admitted in 2022 Was the Highest in the Last 10 Years" ["Число принятых в 2022 году аспирантов стало максимальным за последние 10 лет"], Vedomosti [Ведомости], May 16, 2023.

Herspring, Dale R. "Undermining Combat Readiness in the Russian Military, 1992–2005," *Armed Forces & Society*, Vol. 32, No. 4, July 2006.

Hurska, Alla, "Generation Z: Russia's Militarization of Children," *Eurasia Daily Monitor*, Vol. 20, No. 134, August 18, 2023.

"'I Go to War in My Sleep': Russia Is Failing to Provide PTSD Support for Soldiers Returning from Ukraine. Psychiatrists Expect Disaster," trans. by Sam Breazeale, Meduza, January 26, 2023.

International Institute for Strategic Studies, *The Military Balance*, Routledge, 2022.

Ivshina, Olga [Ившина, Ольга], "More Than 20,000 Identified Dead: What Is Known About Russian Losses in Ukraine by April" ["Более 20 000 установленных погибших: чтоизвестно о потерях России в Украине к апрелю"], BBC Russian Service [BBC Русская служба], April 14, 2023.

Jones, Seth G., Riley McCabe, and Alexander Palmer, *Ukrainian Innovation in a War of Attrition*, Center for Strategic and International Studies, February 27, 2023.

Kanal13, "Russian Soldiers Refuses to Comply with Command Order," video, YouTube, March 30, 2023. As of April 24, 2023: https://www.youtube.com/watch?v=IyVXHzE8tnM

Kates, Glenn, "In Russia, Ukraine Conflict Hits Home with Secret Funerals, Missing Men," Radio Free Europe/Radio Liberty, August 28, 2014.

Khurshudyan, Isabelle, and Michael Robinson Chavez, "Ukrainian Villagers Describe Cruel and Brutal Russian Occupation," *Washington Post*, April 4, 2022.

Kinetz, Erika, "'Never Saw Such Hell': Russian Soldiers in Ukraine Call Home," Associated Press, February 24, 2023.

Kinetz, Erika, Oleksandr Stashevskyi, and Vasilisa Stepanenko, "How Russian Soldiers Ran a 'Cleansing' Operation in Bucha, Ukraine," PBS, November 3, 2022.

Kjellén, Jonas, *Bringing the Soldier Back In: Russian Military Manning, Manpower, and Mobilisation in the Light of Russia's War in Ukraine*, Swedish Defence Research Agency, March 2023.

Klimenko, Ludmila Vladislavovna [Клименко, Людмила Владиславовна], and Oksana Yurievna Posukhova [Оксана Юрьевна Посухова], "Russian Military Personnel Under Institutional Reforms: Professional Attitudes and Identity" ["Российские военнослужащие в условиях институциональных реформ: профессиональные установки и идентичность"], *Journal of Institutional Studies* [Журнал Институциональных Исследований], Vol. 10, No. 2, June 2018.

Kondratyev, Nikita [Кондратьев, Никита], "'The Soldiers Looked at the Political Officer as a Savior and Went to Die'" ["'Солдаты смотрели на замполита как на спасителя и шли умирать'"], *Novaya Gazeta Europe* [Новой газеты Европа], February 28, 2023.

Konstantinova, Alla, "'Teach Kids . . . So That They Are Proud of the War.' Russian School Children Threatened with Expulsion for Refusing to Attend 'Important Conversations,'" Mediazona, September 14, 2022.

Kostarnova, Natalia [Костарнова, Наталья], "Posttraumatic Stress Disorder" ["Посттравматическое стрессовое устройство"], *Kommersant* [*Коммерсантъ*], March 19, 2023.

Krutov, Mark [@kromark], "Soldiers from the 1st Motor Rifle Regiment, part of elite Russian unit, 2nd Guards Tamanskaya Motor Rifle Division (Kalininets, Moscow region) . . . ," post on the X platform, September 12, 2022. As of December 4, 2023:
https://twitter.com/kromark/status/1569395756481806337

Kurbanov, R. R. [Курбанов, Р. Р.], "Monetary Benefit of the Contemporary Military Service Member" ["Денежное довольствие современного военнослужащего"], *Meridian* [*Меридиан*], Vol. 18, 2020.

Lakstygal, Ilya [Лакстыгал, Илья], and Anastasia Mayer [Анастасия Майер], "The Program of Psychological Assistance to Veterans of the Special Operation Is Planned to Be Expanded" ["Программу психологической помощи участникам спецоперации планируют расширить"], Vedemosti [Ведомости], March 20, 2023.

Layout [Вёрстка], Mobilized complaint [Мобилизованные жалуются], post on Telegram, March 9, 2023. As of May 1, 2023:
https://t.me/svobodnieslova/1566

Lee, Rob [@RALee85], "Photos from a destroyed Russian convoy in Chernihiv . . . ," post on the X platform, March 9, 2022. As of December 5, 2023:
https://x.com/RALee85/status/1501631349580521487

Luhn, Alec, "They Were Never There: Russia's Silence for Families of Troops Killed in Ukraine," *The Guardian*, January 19, 2015.

Luzin, Pavel, "New Draft and Mobilization Rules in Russia: Increased Coercion," *Eurasia Daily Monitor*, Vol. 20, No. 121, July 27, 2023.

Main Intelligence Directorate [Головне Управління Розвідки], "List of Personnel of the 20th Guards Motorized Rifle Division of the Armed Forces of the Russian Federation" ["Список особового складу 20-ї гвардійської мотострілецької дивізії ЗС РФ], Ministry of Defense Ukraine [Міністерства Оборони України], March 2, 2022.

Main Intelligence Directorate [Головне Управління Розвідки], "War Criminals—Servicemen of the 136th Separate Motorized Rifle Brigade Committing War Crimes Against the Civilian Population of Ukraine" ["Военные преступники—военнослужащие 136 отдельной мотострелковой бригады совершающие военные преступления против мирного населения Украины"], Ministry of Defense Ukraine [Міністерства Оборони України], March 18, 2022.

Makarov, Dmitriy [Макаров, Дмитрий], "Contract Signed? [Есть контракт]," *Flag of the Motherland* [*Флаг родины*], July 9, 2013.

Malek, Martin, "Russia's Asymmetric Wars in Chechnya Since 1994," *Connections*, Vol. 8, No. 4, Fall 2009.

Massicot, Dara, "What Russia Got Wrong," *Foreign Affairs*, March/April 2023.

McGlynn, Jade [@DrJadeMcGlynn], "Moscow billboard: Images of Soviet WWII heroes montaged with images of modern-day Russian soldiers in Ukraine," post on the X platform, February 19, 2023. As of December 4, 2023: https://twitter.com/DrJadeMcGlynn/status/1627441525578686464

"Military Conscription," Levada-Center, July 13, 2021.

"Military Service Readiness and Hazing" ["Готовность к службе в армии и неуставные отношения"], VTsIOM [ВЦИОМ], December 21, 2020.

"Military Threat" ["Военная Угроза"], Levada-Center [Левада-Центр], January 30, 2019.

Miller, Greg, Mary Ilyushina, Catherine Belton, Isabelle Khurshudyan, and Paul Sonne, "'Wiped Out': War in Ukraine Has Decimated a Once Feared Russian Brigade," *Washington Post*, December 16, 2022.

Mills, Laura, "Russian Conscripts Tell of Fears of Being Sent to Ukraine," Associated Press, February 21, 2015.

Ministry of Defence [@DefenceHQ], "INTELLIGENCE UPDATE: Russia retains a significant military presence that can conduct an invasion without further warning," post on the X platform, February 17, 2022. As of April 4, 2023: https://twitter.com/DefenceHQ/status/1494315294382297091

Ministry of Defence [@DefenceHQ], "Latest Defence Intelligence update on the situation in Ukraine—20 January 2023. Find out more about the UK government's response: http://ow.ly/sUUI50MvNFH," post on the X platform, January 20, 2023a. As of April 15, 2024: https://twitter.com/DefenceHQ/status/1616323761392812033

Ministry of Defence [@DefenceHQ], "Latest Defence Intelligence update on the situation in Ukraine—17 February 2023. Find out more about the UK government's response: http://ow.ly/JtaU50MUSPj," post on the X platform, February 17, 2023b. As of May 28, 2024: https://x.com/DefenceHQ/status/1626472945089486848

Ministry of Defense of the Russian Federation [Министерство обороны Российской Федерации], "Action Plan 2013–2020: Improving the Quality of Troop Training" ["План деятельности на 2013-2020 гг: повышение качества подготовки войск"], undated-a.

Ministry of Defense of the Russian Federation [Министерство обороны Российской Федерации], "Combat Readiness" ["Боеспособность"], undated-b.

Ministry of Defense of the Russian Federation [Министерство обороны Российской Федерации], "On the Results of Performance of the Ministry of Defense of the Russian Federation in 2016" ["Итоги деятельности Министерства обороны Российской Федерации в 2016 году"], undated-c.

Ministry of Defense of the Russian Federation [Министерство обороны Российской Федерации], "Russian Army: Social Problems and Ways to Solve Them" ["Российская армия: социальные проблемы и способы их решения"], undated-d.

Ministry of Defense of the Russian Federation [Министерство обороны Российской Федерации], "Social Benefits Package of the Contract Service Member" ["Социальный пакет военнослужащего-контрактника"], undated-e.

Ministry of Defense of the Russian Federation [Министерство обороны Российской Федерации], "Testimony of the Minister of Defense of the Russian Federation General of the Army Sergei Shoigu at the Russian Defense Ministry Board Session" ["Выступление Министра обороны Российской Федерации генерала армии С.К. Шойгу на расширенном заседании Коллегии Миногороны России"], December 22, 2016.

Ministry of Defense of the Russian Federation [Министерство обороны Российской Федерации], "An Extended Meeting of the Board of the Ministry of Defense Was Held in Moscow Under the Leadership of the Supreme Commander-in-Chief of the Russian Armed Forces Vladimir Putin" ["В Москве состоялось расширенное заседание коллегии Минобороны под руководством Верховного Главнокомандующего Вооружёнными Силами России Владимира Путина"], December 21, 2021.

Ministry of Defense of the Russian Federation [Министерство обороны Российской Федерации], "BARS Reservists Will Gather in 12 Regions of Siberia, the Urals and the Volga Region" ["В 12 регионах Сибири, Урала и Поволжья состоятся Резервисты БАРС соберутся"], January 17, 2022.

Ministry of Defense of Ukraine, "The Total Combat Losses of the Enemy from 24.02.2022 to 28.04.2023," database, April 28, 2023. As of April 28, 2023:
https://www.mil.gov.ua/en/news/2023/04/28/
the-total-combat-losses-of-the-enemy-from-24-02-2022-to-28-04-2023/

"More Than 470 Thousand People Received a Deferment or Exemption from the Army During the Autumn Conscription" ["Более 470 тыс. человек получили отсрочку или освобождение от армии в ходе осеннего призыва"], TASS [ТАСС], January 11, 2017.

Moscow Mayor's Office [Официальный сайт Мэра Москвы], "How to Enroll in Military Service Under a Contract" ["Военная служба по контракту"], webpage, undated. As of December 8, 2023:
https://contract.mos.ru/

Moskos, Charles C., "Institutional/Occupational Trends in Armed Forces: An Update," *Armed Forces & Society*, Vol. 12, No. 3, Spring 1986.

Moskos, Charles C., Jr., "From Institution to Occupation: Trends in Military Organization," *Armed Forces & Society*, Vol. 4, No. 1, Fall 1977.

"'My Soul Is in My Own Hands': The Case of the First Russian Officer Charged with a Felony for Refusing to Kill in Ukraine," trans. by Anna Razumnaya, Meduza, December 27, 2022.

NBC News, "Russian Defense Minister Announces Withdrawal of Troops from Kherson," video, YouTube, November 9, 2022. As of March 12, 2023:
https://www.youtube.com/watch?v=XDlTaMXdnV4

NBC News, "Russian Military Encourages 'Real Men' to Step Forward in Recruitment Ad," video, YouTube, April 21, 2023. As of May 9, 2023:
https://www.youtube.com/watch?v=W_tm6_-mOy8

Nechepurenko, Ivan, and John Ismay, "Russian Lawmakers Toughen Penalties for Soldiers as Moscow Appears to Signal a Possible Escalation," *New York Times*, September 20, 2022.

Newsman [@Taygainfo], post on Telegram, September 1, 2023. As of September 1, 2023:
https://t.me/Taygainfo/41394

NSU [НГУ] [@ng_ukraine], "Hungry Russian soldiers steal chickens from a private household in #Ukraine," post on the X platform, March 9, 2022. As of March 15, 2023:
https://twitter.com/ng_ukraine/status/1501595777814212612

Oliker, Olga, *Russia's Chechen Wars 1994–2000: Lessons from Urban Combat*, RAND Corporation, MR-1289-A, 2001. As of December 5, 2023:
https://www.rand.org/pubs/monograph_reports/MR1289.html

"One Hundred Convictions a Week. Over Two Thousand AWOL Cases Went to Courts in the First Half of 2023, Primarily Against Mobilised Soldiers" ["Сто приговоров в неделю. За полгода в суды поступило больше двух тысяч дел о самоволке—в основном против мобилизованных"], Mediazona [Медиазона], July 19, 2023.

Orlova, Alisa, "Mobilization in Russia: Pertinent Details," *Kyiv Post*, September 21, 2022a.

Orlova, Katerina, "'Freeing Them from the Motherland's Tenacious Grip. Russian Soldiers Are Refusing to Fight in Ukraine. Lawyer Maxim Grebenyuk Is Helping Defend Their Rights," trans. by Sian Glaessner, Meduza, May 3, 2022b.

Osborn, Andrew, "Putin Backs Push for Mercenary Groups to Sign Contracts Despite Wagner's Refusal," Reuters, June 13, 2023.

Pankratieva, Elena [Панкратьева, Елена], "'Without Reading It, They Sign.' Committee of Soldiers' Mothers—About How 18-Year-Olds End Up in Military Service, and About Increasing Their Service Life" ["'Не вчитываясь, ставят подпись.' Комитет солдатских матерей—о том, как 18-летние попадают на СВО, и об увеличении срока службы"], Chita.RU [Чита.РУ], November 14, 2022.

Pavlova, Anna, "When Soldiers Say No. Hundreds of Russian Servicemen Face Trial in Defiance of Ukraine Deployment, Mediazona Study Reveals," Mediazona, April 11, 2023.

Pavlova, Valentina [Павлова, Валентина], "Motivation of Volunteers for Contract Military Service" ["Мотивация добровольцев на военную службу по контракту"], *Russian Military Review* [*Российское военное обозрение*], Vol. 11, No. 46, November 2007.

PBS NewsHour, "Defense Secretary Austin and Gen. Milley Hold News Conference in Germany," video, YouTube, January 20, 2023. As of May 1, 2023:
https://www.youtube.com/watch?v=kaIuWizss9o&t=350s

Penchansky, Roy, and J. William Thomas, "The Concept of Access: Definition and Relationship to Consumer Satisfaction," *Medical Care*, Vol. 19, No. 2, February 1981.

Petrova, Yana [Петрова, Яна], "PTSD After the War in Chechnya" ["ПТСР после войны в Чечне"], Pikabu [Пикабу], July 1, 2021.

President of Russia, "Meeting with First Deputy Speaker of the Federation Council Andrei Turchak," Presidential Executive Office, April 24, 2023.

"Prigozhin Says More Than 5,000 Former Prisoners Have Been Freed After Serving in Wagner Group," Meduza, March 26, 2023.

Prince, Todd, "Sweetening a Bitter Pill: Russia Offers Debt Breaks, Other Benefits to Entice Draftees," *Radio Free Europe/Radio Liberty*, September 28, 2022a.

Prince, Todd, "A Russian Father Left His Family Decades Ago. Now He Wants Half His Dead Son's Ukraine War Compensation," *Radio Free Europe/Radio Liberty*, November 11, 2022b.

"Putin Signs Law Raising Maximum Draft Age," *Moscow Times*, August 4, 2023.

"Putin Signs Law to Mobilize Russians Who Committed Serious Crimes— RIA," *Jerusalem Post*, November 4, 2022.

"Putin Promised Those Fighting in Ukraine Priority Hiring for Civil Service" ["Путин пообещал воюющим в Украине приоритетный наём на госслужбу"], *Moscow Times Russian Service*, February 21, 2023.

"Putin Toughens Punishments for 'Discrediting' Russian Military," *Kyiv Independent*, March 18, 2023.

Putin, V. [Путин, В.], "On the Creation of the State Fund for Supporting Participants in the Special Military Operation 'Defenders of the Fatherland'" ["О Создании Государственного Фонда Поддержки Участников Специальной Военной Операции 'Защитники Отечества'"], Decree of the President of the Russian Federation [Указ Президента Российской Федерации], *Guardian of the Baltic* [*Страж Балтики*], Vol. 12, April 7, 2023.

Quinn, Allison, "Russia Used Beatings and Tricks to Forcibly Send Rookie Troops to Ukraine, Rights Group Says," Daily Beast, February 24, 2022a.

Quinn, Allison, "'There Is Such F---ery Going on Here': Russian Soldiers 'Revolting' as They Get Stiffed on Ukraine Payouts," Daily Beast, April 13, 2022b.

Raschepkin, Konstantin [Ращепкин, Константин], and Viktor Pyakov [Виктор Пьяков], "The Path to Professionalism" ["Путь в профессионалы"], *On Duty* [*На боевом посту*], Vols. 69–70, 2008.

Renz, Bettina, *Russia's Military Revival*, Polity Press, 2018.

Romashova, Olya, "'I Don't Know How Else to Get Through to Our Government': A Russian Arsonist Explains His Thinking," trans. by Sam Breazeale, Meduza, October 18, 2022.

Rosenberg, Steven, "Ukraine Crisis: Forgotten Death of Russian Soldier," BBC News, September 18, 2014.

Rozhanskiy, Timofei, "Why Russian Soldiers Are Refusing to Fight in the War in Ukraine," Radio Free Europe/Radio Liberty, July 20, 2022.

Rubin, Elizabeth, "'Only You Can Save Your Sons,'" *New York Times*, July 8, 2001.

"Russia Calls Up 300,000 Reservists, Says 6,000 Soldiers Killed in Ukraine," Reuters, September 21, 2022.

"Russia Elevated Requirements for Conscript Health" ["В России повысили требования к здоровью призывников"], RIA News [РИА Новости], September 9, 2021.

"Russia Expands War Recruitment Drive with Video Calling for 'Real' Men," NDTV, April 20, 2023.

"Russia Sends Mobilized Men to Ukraine Front After Days of Training— Activists," *Moscow Times*, September 27, 2022.

"Russia Toughens Penalty for Voluntary Surrender, Refusal to Fight," Radio Free Europe/Radio Liberty, September 24, 2022.

"Russian Army," Levada-Center, December 16, 2022.

"Russian Casualties in Ukraine. Mediazona Summary" ["Потери России в войне с Украиной. Сводка Медиазоны"], Mediazona [Медиазона], webpage, updated December 1, 2023. As of December 4, 2023: https://zona.media/casualties

"Russian Duma Approves Bill Raising Age Limit for Military Personnel to 65," Radio Free Europe/Radio Liberty, May 25, 2022.

"Russian FSB Approves New List of Information That Could Pose National Security Threat," Meduza, October 1, 2021.

"Russians Have Adapted to HIMARS. What Are Ukraine's Alternatives?" *Euromaidan Press*, January 9, 2023.

"Russia's Vanished Combatants: Thousands of Russian Servicemen Are MIA in Ukraine. Most of Them Are Likely Dead, but Their Families Can Neither Bury Them nor File for State Compensation," Meduza, February 28, 2023.

Rustamova, Farida, and Maxim Tovkaylo, "Anything but More Mobilization: Russia's Stealthy Push to Find More Soldiers," *Moscow Times*, April 6, 2023.

Ryan, Kevin, "Is the Russian Military Running Out of Soldiers?" Harvard Kennedy School Belfer Center for Science and International Affairs, Russia Matters, March 28, 2022.

Ryzhkova, Anna, "'He Survived War but Not Rehabilitation': An Employee at a Rehab Center Describes Caring for Russian Soldiers Returning from the Front," trans. by Emily Laskin, Meduza, March 18, 2023.

Saito, Mari, Maria Tsvetkova, and Anton Zverev, "Abandoned Russian Base Holds Secrets of Retreat in Ukraine," Reuters, October 26, 2022.

Sauer, Pjotr, "Russian Soldiers Say Commanders Used 'Barrier Troops' to Stop Them Retreating," *The Guardian*, March 27, 2023.

Schlottman, Henry [@HN_Schlottman], "Last month, ⬛ military intel posted what appeared to be a complete roster of ⬛ 136th Separate Guards Motorized Rifle Brigade. It helpfully provided info for contract vs conscript personnel (rare) which I've broken down by subunit in this graphic," post on the X platform, April 23, 2022. As of November 1, 2022: https://twitter.com/HN_Schlottman/status/1517895344650166272/photo/1

Schreck, Carl, "'Simply Medieval': Russian Soldiers Held in Pits and Cellars for Refusing to Fight in Ukraine," Radio Free Europe/Radio Liberty, July 15, 2023.

Schwirtz, Michael, Anton Troianovski, Yousur Al-Hlou, Masha Froliak, Adam Entous, and Thomas Gibbons-Neff, "Putin's War," *New York Times*, December 16, 2022.

Security Service of Ukraine [Служба безпеки України], "The occupiers, who have sensed the strength of the ZSU, are preparing their dying laments for their loved ones" ["Окупанти, які відчули силу ЗСУ, готують передсмертні прохання своїм близьким"], post on Telegram, April 8, 2022. As of December 5, 2023: https://t.me/SBUkr/4083

"'Sent There to Be Meat': Why Russian Draftees Are Suddenly Publishing So Many Video Pleas to Putin," trans. by Sam Breazeale, Meduza, March 9, 2023.

Sevrinovsky, Vladimir, "'Refusing to Kill People Isn't a Crime': The Russian National Guard Is Firing Officers Who Refuse to Join the War in Ukraine," trans. by Sam Breazeale, Meduza, March 29, 2022.

Sheftalovich, Zoya, "Full Text of Putin's Mobilization Decree—Translated," Politico, September 21, 2022.

"Shoigu Proposed Increasing the Number of Military Personnel to 1.5 Million" ["Шойгу предложил увеличить численность военнослужащих до 1,5 млн"], RBC [РБК], December 21, 2022.

Siberia.Realities [Сибирь.Реалии], "8,000 Relatives of Those Mobilized Signed a Petition Demanding That Time Limits Be Set for Their Men to Stay in the War in Ukraine" ["8000 родственников мобилизованных подписали петицию с требованием установить предельные сроки пребывания их мужчин на войне в Украине"], post on Telegram, May 5, 2023. As of September 12, 2023: https://t.me/sibrealii/17955

Sidorkova, Inna [Сидоркова, Инна], and Alexander Atasuntsev [Александр Атасунцев], "Who and How Volunteers Are Recruited for Special Military Operations in Ukraine ["Кто и как набирает добровольцев на военную спецоперацию на Украине"], RBC [РБК], July 9, 2022.

Simpson, Michael, Adam R. Grissom, Christopher A. Mouton, John P. Godges, and Russell Hanson, *Road to Damascus: The Russian Air Campaign in Syria, 2015 to 2018*, RAND Corporation, RR-A1170-1, 2022. As of December 5, 2023: https://www.rand.org/pubs/research_reports/RRA1170-1.html

Sivtsova, Sasha, "'We Have No Idea Who We're Fighting For': How Russia Threatens Contract Soldiers Who Refuse to Fight in Ukraine," trans. by Sasha Zibrov, Meduza, May 16, 2022.

Sivtsova, Sasha, and Kristina Safonova, "'I'm Panicking—Where Is My Child?' Conscript Soldiers Are Being Sent to Fight Against Ukraine, Their Relatives Say. Here's What Their Families Told Meduza," trans. by Sam Breazeale, Meduza, February 25, 2022.

Slavin, Alexey, "'What Does Missing in Action Mean? Is My Son Dead?' Meduza Talks to Mothers of Conscripts Who Served Aboard the Sunken Russian Warship Moskva," trans. by Eilish Hart, Meduza, April 20, 2022.

Solugub, Nikita, "'I'm F---ing Done with This Army.' Russian Military Stunned as Mediazona Tells Them Their Secret Calls from Ukraine Published in the New York Times," Mediazona, March 17, 2023.

"The State Duma Allowed the Mobilization of Those Convicted of Serious Crimes" ["Госдума разрешила мобилизацию судимых по тяжким статьям"], Radio Liberty [Радио Свобода], October 27, 2022.

Sutyagin, Igor, "Russian Forces in Ukraine," Royal United Services Institute for Defence and Security Studies, March 2015.

Svetlova, Anna [Светлова, Анна], "There Is Less Hazing and More Corruption in the Russian Armed Forces" ["В российской армии стало меньше дедовщины и больше коррупции"], Gazeta.ru [Газета.Ру], March 10, 2021.

Talanova, Daria [Таланова, Дарья], and Antonina Asanova [Антонина Асанова], "'My Sister and I Visited All the Morgues'" ["'Мы с сестрой обошли все морги'"], *Novaya Gazeta Europe* [*Новой газеты Европа*], February 27, 2023.

Talanova, Daria [Таланова, Дарья], and Nikita Kondratyev [Никита Кондратьев], "Direct Outdoor to the Front" ["Прямая наружка на фронт"], *Novaya Gazeta Europe* [*Новой газеты Европа*], April 18, 2023.

Tenisheva, Anastasia, "'Advocating for War Is Wrong': Russian Teachers Resign over Refusal to Allow Ukraine Veterans in Class," *Moscow Times*, September 7, 2023.

"There Will Be Half a Million Contract Soldiers in the Russian Army" ["В российской армии будет полмиллиона контрактников"], Interfax [Интерфакс], December 18, 2020.

"'They Drink a Lot, Sell Their Fuel': Belarusians Give Low Marks to Russian Troops Deployed for Drills," Radio Free Europe/Radio Liberty, February 19, 2022.

"'They Told Us Nobody's Going to Take Us Home': Russian Soldiers Held Captive in Luhansk Region for Refusing to Fight in Ukraine," Meduza, July 22, 2022.

Tickle, Jonny [@jonnytickle], "This is the flyer they're handing out. According to this, soldiers fighting in the 'Special Military Operation Zone' receive a wage between 210k–340k rubles ($2,500–$4,200) a month," post on the X platform, April 7, 2023. As of April 8, 2023:
https://twitter.com/jonnytickle/status/1644340794516467716

Tiunova, Polina [Тиунова, Полина], "In Chelyabinsk, Doctors Gave Advice on How the Military Can Cope with the Consequences of Combat Psychological Trauma" ["В Челябинске врачи дали советы, как военным справиться с последствиями боевой психологической травмы"], Bezformata [Безформата], October 13, 2022.

Trading Economics, "Russia Average Monthly Wages," database, undated. As of March 3, 2023:
https://tradingeconomics.com/russia/wages

Troianovski, Anton, and Marc Santora, "Growing Evidence of a Military Disaster on the Donets Pierces a Pro-Russian Bubble," *New York Times*, May 15, 2022.

Tumakova, Irina [Тумакова, Ирина], "Mom, I Love You, if There Is a Funeral, Don't Believe It Right Away" ["Мама, я тебя люблю, если будет похоронка, не верь сразу"], UkrRudProm [УкрРудПром], March 4, 2022.

United Nations Human Rights Council, *Report of the Independent International Commission of Inquiry on Ukraine*, A/HRC/52/62, advance unedited version, March 15, 2023.

"UN Predicts Russia's Population Could Halve by 2100," *Moscow Times*, June 18, 2019.

Valchenko, Sergey [Вальченко, Сергей], "The Expert Warned About Possible Psychological Problems of Veterans of the SVO" ["Эксперт предупредила о возможных психологических проблемах участников СВО"], Moskovsky Komsomolets [Московский Комсомолец], December 2, 2022.

Vasilyev, Pavel, "Across the Minefields. Eight Mobilised Russian Soldiers Fled the War Zone in Ukraine and Were Accused of Desertion," Mediazona, February 5, 2023.

Vendil Pallin, Carolina, *Russian Military Reform: A Failed Exercise in Defence Decision Making*, Routledge, 2009.

Vkladka, Novaya, "'They Drink Out of Fear': A Dispatch from the Closed Russian Military Village Where Six Draftees Have Died Since Mobilization Began," trans. by Sam Breazeale, Meduza, February 22, 2023.

Voron, Bogdan [@Bogdan_Voron], "The Ukrainian army servicemen found a pile of 'refusers' reports . . . ," post on the X platform, September 19, 2022. As of December 5, 2023:
https://twitter.com/bogdan_voron/status/1571862546927206400

WarTranslated (Dmitri) [@wartranslated], "Another group of Russian mobiks lost in Ukraine," post on the X platform, February 18, 2023a. As of September 12, 2023:
https://x.com/wartranslated/status/1626870604258328577

WarTranslated (Dmitri) [@wartranslated], "Russian women appeal to Putin for assistance with their mobilised men—in this new video . . . ," May 21, 2023b. As of September 12, 2023:
https://twitter.com/wartranslated/status/1660296610088189954

"'We Were Nothing to Them': Russian Volunteer Reservists Return from War Against Ukraine Feeling Deceived," Radio Free Europe/Radio Liberty, August 12, 2022.

"What Benefits Are Provided for SVO Participants? Graphic Arts" ("Какие льготы предусмотрены для участников СВО. Графика"], Izvestia [Известия], January 18, 2023.

"Wounded Russian Soldiers Returned to Front Without Proper Treatment— Agentstvo," *Moscow Times*, January 12, 2023.

Wright, George, "Ukraine War: More Than 20,000 Russian Troops Killed Since December, U.S. Says," BBC News, May 1, 2023.

Yapparova, Lilia, "'Not a Single Step Back!' In a Booklet Issued to Soldiers, the Russian Authorities Denounce the Army's 'Shameful' Retreat from Kherson and Urge a Return to 'Stalinist Methods,'" trans. by Sam Breazeale, Meduza, April 5, 2023.

Zabrodskyi, Mykhaylo, Jack Watling, Oleksandr V. Danylyuk, and Nick Reynolds, *Preliminary Lessons in Conventional Warfighting from Russia's Invasion of Ukraine: February–July 2022*, Royal United Services Institute for Defence and Security Studies, November 30, 2022.

Zakharchenko, Kateryna, "Russia Boosts Its Army with 'Voluntarily' Mobilized Students," *Kyiv Post*, December 20, 2023.